Advance Praise

"This is a sweet, insightful account of the life of a school teacher who's simultaneously going through both professional and cultural challenges and approaches the new job with an open mind and an open heart. It's nicely written and well observed, and I felt as if I were going through the daily life in a Baltimore classroom with all of its challenges and little pleasures and large frustrations."

—Michael Olesker, former *Baltimore Sun* columnist and WJZ-TV commentator, and author of six books. His most recent, *Front Stoops in the Fifties: Baltimore Legends Come of Age*, was reissued in paperback by the Johns Hopkins University Press

Forgive Us Our Trespasses

Forgive Us Our Trespasses

A Jewish Teacher in a Catholic School

A Memoir

Diane Gensler

Apprentice
House Press
Loyola University Maryland

First Edition

Casebound ISBN: 978-1-62720-282-4
Paperback ISBN: 978-1-62720-283-1
Ebook ISBN: 978-1-62720-284-8

Printed in the United States of America

Design by Hannah Kozieja
Editorial development by Annabelle Finagin
Promotion by Justus Croyle
Author photo by David Stuck Photography

Published by Apprentice House Press

Apprentice
House Press
Loyola University Maryland

Apprentice House Press
Loyola University Maryland
4501 N. Charles Street
Baltimore, MD 21210
410.617.5265 • 410.617.2198 (fax)
www.ApprenticeHouse.com
info@ApprenticeHouse.com

For my parents who always told me I could be whatever I want

Author's Note

I wrote this book to share my experiences and feelings about teaching as a Jewish person in a Catholic School. It is not my intention to implicate anyone nor lay blame. I changed names and descriptions to protect identities.

Prologue

READ THIS BITCH!

This was the welcome note I received my first day of teaching September 1, 1992 at a local parochial school in my hometown of Baltimore. I found it sitting on my desk before school started. I was startled. Was this meant for me? If so, why was someone calling me the b word? I picked it up, looked closely at the penciled scrawling, and turned it over.

JESUS IS THE MESSIAH AND DON'T YOU FORGET IT!

Now it made sense. This was the greeting I received as a Jewish teacher in a Catholic school. Had they never met a Jew before? Did everyone already know I was Jewish? How? Who could have written such a note?

***

I was in my twenties, and all I wanted to do was teach. In pretend play as a child, I would write questions on my chalkboard and make handouts to give invisible students. When my twelfth grade English teacher went around the room and asked everyone what they wanted to be, I told her I wanted to be her!

When I started babysitting at age thirteen, I knew I loved working with kids. The two sisters from my regular Saturday night babysitting job would beg their parents to go out so I could babysit. We had fun choreographing dances to their favorite music and playing a doodle drawing game I created (that years later appeared in stores). My mother compared me to the Pied Piper because children were drawn to me.

Even though I attended a local college while commuting from home, I became overwhelmed trying to keep up with my coursework, including the general university requirements. I floundered that first year, forgetting my original ambition. In my second year, I took an introductory class called "Careers in Education" which reignited my interest in the field. When I stepped into my first full-fledged education class the next semester, I knew I was where I was meant to be. I declared a double major of English and Secondary Education, and my grade point average improved tremendously since I was now taking classes that really engaged me. For my student teaching internship at the end of my education program, I was paired with an experienced, talented middle school teacher who knew how to bring out the best in me. I relished my time learning from her and the time spent with the students.

Once I graduated, this teacher helped me get a job as a long-term substitute in the same school. I taught for several months in place of the permanent teacher, writing my own lesson plans, grading students' papers, and holding all the responsibilities of the full-time teacher. After the original teacher returned, I did this two more times in two other public schools.

The third time the permanent teacher was to return after winter break. I was so upset about having to leave that on my last day, I was issued a speeding ticket for going 80 mph on the beltway on my way home! I hadn't realized I was accelerating with all the tears in my eyes.

***

I didn't realize my passion would cause such turmoil and anti-Semitism in my first full-length teaching job. In 1992 there was uproar in other areas of the United States. Race relations were tense after Rodney King, a black taxi driver, was beaten ruthlessly by Los Angeles police, causing rioting and political unrest throughout the nation. (Unfortunately history repeated itself in Baltimore in 2015 with the Freddie Gray case.)

The Crown Heights riots from the previous year were still fresh on everyone's minds. In that section of Brooklyn, riots broke out between black and Orthodox Jewish residents after two black children were struck and one of them was killed by the motorcade of a highly respected Orthodox rabbi. Black teenagers even killed a non-Jew thinking he was Jewish.

Also in the same year, the Catholic Church was reeling from multiple allegations of sexual abuse around the country by priests and clergy. It was estimated that at this point, dioceses in the United States had paid out four hundred million dollars in legal fees and reparations. In October, singer and musician Sinead O'Connor, in an appearance on late night television show *Saturday Night Live*, sang her song "War" and tore up a photograph of Pope John Paul II in protest.

A little earlier in April, major Italian-American mob boss, John Gotti, was sentenced to life in prison for his crimes. Watching the news story with his mug shot posted on the screen made me shiver as I realized that characters and evil-doers right out of *Scarface* and *The Godfather* actually exist in this world. Soon I was to encounter some characters that probably would have liked to use Gotti to "put a hit out" on me!

On the heels of the real-life John Gotti drama came a comedy in the movie theatre that gained popularity. Whoopi Goldberg starred in *Sister Act*, playing a nightclub singer who witnesses a mob crime and is forced to hide in a convent. She forms a choir with the nuns.

I didn't realize at the time that I'd soon be teaching in a Catholic school, although the teacher nuns I encountered had all retired from the order. My experience there would be anything but comical.

***

I was finally starting the job of my dreams. I couldn't wait to get to my own classroom that first day of school. I had practiced what I was going to say to the students so many times that I was probably mumbling, "Good morning, class" in my sleep. I set my alarm an hour earlier than necessary, awoke several times before the alarm, fell back to sleep, and when it went off again, jumped up like a fire fighter responding to a call.

Several weeks before, I had chosen a white, floral skirt suit, an outfit I considered to be a combination of regality and professionalism. I felt I could have been running for President of the United States or having tea with the Queen of England. I had worn this outfit several times to religious services at my synagogue. Pink flowers, leaves and long, intertwining stems ran rampant over the white short-sleeved, puffy-shouldered jacket and matching straight skirt. In hindsight, I may have appeared as one big sapling from head to foot.

I was finished with roommates and lived happily by myself in a top floor apartment on the outskirts of the city. After a twenty minute drive to school, it was 7:00 a.m. when I pulled into the parking lot in my parents' hand-me-down silver Dodge Aries sedan. The season had changed to fall, the sky was clear, and there was a slight breeze. I was so excited I was coatless and oblivious to the crispness of the early morning hour. I secured the parking spot closest to the door, since I was the only car in the front lot.

When I turned the handle of the front door to the building, my exhaled breath clouded the air, as I was relieved to find it was unlocked. I noticed the front office was vacant, although the lights were on. I felt comforted that somebody else, even if it was a maintenance person, was in the building. I continued through the lobby, turned right, and proceeded down the long, dark corridor that led to my classroom. The school was organized with the younger grades down the hallway to the left, and the older grades down the hallway to the right. I was teaching sixth, seventh, and eighth grade English Language Arts, and my homeroom class consisted of sixth graders. My room was a distance down the hall.

I passed the unlit classrooms of the third, fourth, and fifth grades. All it would have taken was for someone to open one of those doors and shout "BOO!" and I would have run screaming back to the front door. If the symphonic music with the chanted Latin lyrics from *The Omen* was playing and cobwebs and candlebras adorned the hall, the place would have been ready for Halloween. There was a light at the far end of the hallway past all the classrooms. Its source was from a connection to another building with which I was unfamiliar, but I was grateful for the illumination. I told myself to walk toward the light. Ironically, I found out later it was a hallway that led to the church.

I carried my brown leather briefcase with a combination lock that was a college graduation gift from my aunt and uncle. I was happy to finally use it. It contained my grade book, seating charts, lesson plans, unit plans, handouts, and transparencies. I had already prepared for the next few months using materials I had taken home. It didn't take me long in the weeks ahead to realize I needed to graduate to something larger in order to carry all the paperwork I amassed.

I walked down the last small set of stairs and arrived at my classroom on the left. I swung open the door, turned on the lights, and stood there taking it all in.

The room looks terrific! My students should feel welcome, and we should all feel comfortable. I love my bulletin boards that I put so much time into creating and putting up myself. I love the room arrangement. I'm ready. This classroom was meant for me. It was designated to no one else but me. Here is where in the coming months I will be making a difference in children's lives. Here is the place where I will spend most of my waking hours. Bring on the kids!

The school had been in existence since the 1950s, but some classrooms were added later and then refurbished in the eighties. You could tell the school was a combination of old and new. My classroom looked upgraded from a public school classroom because it had mauve carpet (albeit not lavish or lush but rather worn and faded), a long row of windows which overlooked a small expanse of lawn, a separate section of hooks for coats and backpacks behind a painted pink cinder block wall, a relatively large walk-in closet on the far side of the room by my desk, and a separate exit door in case of emergency. I had already grown accustomed to the sculptured head of the Virgin Mary mounted like an animal trophy above the chalkboard at the front of the room. (No offense intended here; it's just that it felt really "in my face.")

I had been in the school almost every day in the weeks prior for faculty meetings and planning time, so I had plenty of time to decorate and arrange my room. A day or two before, I had written on the blackboard my objectives and directions in my careful, precise script. My overhead projector and transparencies awaited on a cart in the front of the room facing the pull-down screen. My handouts for the day were stacked neatly in my closet and ready to go.

Standing in the doorway, I glanced around the room. Then I noticed the index card on my desk.

Someone is certainly sending a message, I thought. *Someone definitely doesn't want me here.*

I kept staring at the note. When the fog in my head cleared a little, I became offended over being called a bitch more than about not accepting Jesus Christ as my savior. It looked like a child's handwriting.

If a kid wrote this, what could have prompted it?

I couldn't be angry if it was a child, because that just shows blatant ignorance. But even if it was a child, ultimately the sentiment would come from an adult. And that thought made me angry.

I didn't have long to ponder this because I was interrupted by Mrs. A, the teacher who taught English Language Arts directly across the hall. They called her my "teaching partner" because she taught the other half of the sixth, seventh, and eighth grades, not because we were assigned to work together. When we were introduced, I was told she taught the above-average students, and I would get the students who were lower ability.

Mrs. H, the religion teacher and a former nun, had stopped by my classroom in one of the first weeks of school.

"How are you doing?" she asked.

"I'm good," I answered. I was glad someone cared enough to check on me.

"Do you know why you got all the low kids?" she asked.

"No," I answered. I hadn't thought about it.

"Because Mrs. A doesn't want them. She always teaches the higher students. She's been here a long time, and the principal gives her what she wants."

"Oh," I responded, unsure of what to say to that.

"I think I heard her once call them 'the bottom of the barrel.' She doesn't want to teach them. Just thought you might want to know."

"Okay," I said. "Thank you."

She whisked herself down the hall before I could ask her anything.

Wow. The bottom of the barrel? How can you ever say that about any child? Each child is unique and has something to offer. I love all kids. How can a teacher even utter those words?

Mrs. A seemed nicer than that. She did have the more advanced students though. I didn't want to make any harsh judgments about her. She seemed to be an accomplished teacher, and I had to work with her the whole year. I didn't want to be prejudiced against her at the very start. Although I couldn't see how the religion teacher would fabricate such a story. I would just have to ignore this comment for now.

Mrs. A was a tall, slender, redhead in her forties, her face sunburnt from time spent gardening in her backyard. She told me she found it relaxing to spend time digging in the soil. In my mind I could see her like Wilma in "The Flintstones" Hannah Barbera cartoons, thrusting her raptor-footed trowel into the ground, heaving it over her shoulder, and covering Fred in dirt.

Her hair was pulled back with a large clip. It looked effortless but professional. In spite of her youthful appearance, I considered the hairstyle a modern version of the old-fashioned schoolmarm. When we had met for the first time, she had flashed her broad, sparkling Cheshire cat smile.

"I saw your light on, so I came over," Mrs. A explained.

I was surprised to see her, as it was still very early and I thought I was the only teacher in the building. She asked what I was holding in my hand. It was several minutes after I found the note, but I hadn't moved. I was still standing in front of my desk. I showed her the card.

She took it from me. As she read, she scrunched up her face like someone who just smelled a rotten egg. She turned the card over, read the back, and then re-examined both sides.

"Somebody left this on your desk?"

"Yes," I answered nodding.

"Why would somebody do that?" she asked rhetorically. "The handwriting looks familiar, but I can't place it." She paused. "I'll take this to Mr. Z."

She strutted off in her medium-heeled sandals and pearl necklace to the principal's office. I wondered why she didn't suggest I take the card to him. But then I figured it might be better if I didn't have to deal with it. I assumed she was trying to be helpful.

I later asked her what the principal said.

"He said he would keep the card and investigate."

Investigate? That sounds like a week or more of lost time. Doesn't this demand immediate attention? Shouldn't he come out of his office and deal with this now? Perhaps he could call an assembly and discuss this situation with the entire school. Do they not care that a brand new teacher is being harassed? How were they planning on investigating? Were they going to interview students? Were they going to do handwriting comparisons? Why would you let this wait and let the trail go cold? These thoughts were now screaming through my head.

As far as I knew, no one was on the case. A few weeks later I asked Mrs. A about it, and she told me that she hadn't heard anything. When I told her I was thinking of talking about it directly with the principal, she said there was no need. But I did ask if he had learned anything when I was in his office several months later over another matter.

"I haven't discovered anything," he answered with a snarl that reminded me of a bulldog protecting its territory.

For the remainder of the school year no one mentioned it. I inquired again toward the end of the year, and Mrs. A told me she still hadn't heard anything. I regretted having shared the incident with her at all.

Eventually the truth came to light on one of the last days of school. I was able to face the perpetrators, at least those of the juvenile kind. It was the adults who concerned me more, for they had made my entire school year miserable. Never have I felt as though I faced so much anti-Semitism and prejudice, especially in an institution that declares itself to be so spiritual, loving and accepting. Looking back, in some ways I was rather naive from the start. I believe the juvenile wrongdoers eventually regretted their actions and truly learned to be tolerant of all cultures. The adults, however, did not seem to learn that lesson.

Chapter 1

Our Father, who art in Heaven

My counselor at Jewish Vocational Services suggested I apply for a teaching position in a private or parochial school.

"Teaching is teaching no matter where you do it," she said.

After my long-term substitute experiences, I took work as a temporary secretary for several years. I enjoyed helping out in various offices, but I had been doing it for so long it was starting to feel permanent. I hadn't given up my dream of becoming a full-time teacher, and I needed guidance. Despite all my experience in the public school system, the county still hadn't come calling, even after the extensive interview process.

I had been working with my counselor for many months, and I trusted her judgment. In addition, the next school year was approaching rapidly.

Even though I knew I was a teacher through and through, she still put me through a barrage of personality, interest and aptitude tests. The results were always the same, showing an inclination for teaching.

The Meyers-Briggs Type Indicator classified me as an ISFJ /ESFJ (Introverted and Extroverted, Sensing, Feeling, Judging). This type of person is sympathetic and concerned with people. It was no surprise that teaching is listed as a possible career along with secretarial work, library work, counseling, and a few others.

The Strong Interest Inventory results read that I "have specifically defined interests in the following basic areas: writing, office practices and teaching." How accurate is that?!

The Kuder Preference Record gave me a high score in literary interest which lists the jobs of novelist, historian, teacher, actor, news reporter, editor, drama critic, librarian and book reviewer. Except for news reporter, all of these jobs are "right on the money!"

There was no denying that teaching was my calling, so my counselor focused on pursuing only teaching positions.

On her advice, I answered a help wanted ad for a local parochial school. A week or so later I was sitting in the principal's office for an interview. It was almost 100 degrees that August day, as I sat there in my interview outfit—a white shirt beneath a long-sleeved collarless red button down jacket, a long black skirt, nude panty hose, and black patent leather dress shoes. My long, curly hair was down, covering my neck and shoulders.

"Sorry the air conditioning is broken," Mr. Z began, gesturing to the noiseless unit in the window. "Feel free to make yourself more comfortable." He looked at me as though he expected me to unbutton my jacket.

I didn't move a muscle, literally, as I was afraid to even change positions. They say you only get seven seconds to make a good first impression. My seven seconds were up, but I wasn't taking any chances.

"I'm fine," I responded, as the nylon stuck to my legs which stuck to his black leather sofa. I really wanted to kick off my shoes, rip off my hose and tear off my blazer. But I was focused only on getting this job. My dedication to teaching and my fortitude for wanting this job must have shown in my willingness to take a sweat bath in my clothes.

Mr. Z started by telling me that he is not a member of the clergy but a lay person.

A member of the clergy? What's that? Oh, a priest or minister, I suppose. Why would he be that? Oh, I guess some prinicpals are. I didn't expect him to be.

After he asked me a few general questions, he explained that he was looking for a language arts teacher for one class each for grades 6, 7, and 8.

Oh dear. That's three separate lesson plans every day.

I knew that was a tremendous amount of work. I had taught five different ability levels of one grade for one subject, and even that was a challenge. But I smiled and indicated I was still interested.

At one point, Mr. Z read from the contract I would have to sign if I took the job. It was a list of qualities he was looking for in the teacher he was hiring, and one of the items said, "Displays Christian values."

"I'm not Christian," I said.

14

"Yes," he responded.

Yes? Does he already know? How? I know by law he's not allowed to ask what my religion is. I'm going to keep my mouth shut. I think it's better if I don't say anything. I really want this job, and if I tell him, then I may not get it even though that's discrimination. Am I making a mistake? Perhaps I should tell him and get it out in the open. No, I don't think so. I'm not going to volunteer that I'm Jewish. Although I think he knows.

Perhaps it was my last name. Or perhaps it was my curly hair and long nose. Maybe he and his staff could sniff us out like detection dogs they use for drugs. Maybe he was descended from Nazis, so it was in his blood to ferret us out. Or perhaps it was all in my head and I was imagining that he already knew.

"That won't be a problem," he answered. You don't have to be a Christian to display Christian values."

"Oh," was all I could muster. I'd have to let that sink in.

"How many applicants do you have for this position?" I asked.

"Two others," he answered. "One is a social studies teacher, but she would be okay teaching English. The other is an elementary school teacher."

"You don't want them; you want me!" I declared, more boldly than ever in my life. "I'm the secondary English language arts teacher you are looking for."

Did I really just say that?

Honestly, I didn't think that neither a social studies teacher with no experience teaching English nor an elementary school teacher would do well teaching English in a middle school.

Perhaps it was my declaration that helped, because he offered me the job at the end of the interview. I accepted right away, even though the salary was a mere $17,000 a year.

He sent me to the school office with paperwork to complete and told me to see the secretary. She wasn't hard to find, as there was only one. She stopped typing on her brown IBM electric typewriter to ask me how she could help. I told her what I needed, and she directed me to pull up a chair to her desk.

After a few minutes of filling out forms, she pushed her reading glasses down her nose, looked at me, and said, "I noticed that you aren't Catholic."

How does she know that? Maybe the principal checked off "none of the above" under Catholic religious denominations.

"I'm as far away from Catholic as you can be," I replied, thinking that Judaism was the opposite extreme since I knew absolutely nothing about Catholicism.

"You're Jewish?"

I nodded. She must have drawn that conclusion from my previous statement. The question itself was making me perspire even more.

"Jews actually have a lot in common with Catholics, more so than some other religions," she said smiling. "You'd be surprised."

I felt somewhat relieved, as this could have gone several different ways — She could have shredded my paperwork and told me to leave, marched to the principal's office and asked if he was insane, or interrogated me and asked if I knew what I was doing, which I was beginning to wonder at this point.

Instead she said, "Don't worry. We're glad you're here."

This made me feel welcome. It wouldn't take long to find how mistaken I was.

Chapter 2

Hallowed Be Thy Name

It was a week before school started, and I sat at a science lab table in a faculty meeting with all the teachers from pre-K to the upper school. I was acquainted with the middle school teachers since I would be working the closest with them. It felt as if we were paired up like Noah's Ark since there were two homeroom teachers for each middle school grade. The two eighth grade homeroom teachers appeared to be best friends, and the two seventh grade homeroom teachers were both former nuns and seemed well-acquainted.

Most of the teachers had been teaching there for years and, at some point, had their own children enrolled. They would get a steep tuition discount which sounded like a good deal. Mrs. A's son had graduated the previous year.

Mr. Z led the meeting. He was a tall, dark-haired, clean-cut, suited gentleman who looked to be about the same age as Mrs. A. He had been the principal for the past several years, was well-liked, and had a good reputation. As I had learned, Mrs. A was friendly with him and was frequently in his office.

There was a lot of chatter, so he asked everyone to quiet down. He made the meeting brief, as it lasted only a half hour. Within that time he gave us our official schedules, student lists, and miscellaneous information about how the school year would run. As I held my list of students, a wave of anxiety washed over me like someone had just poured cold water down my back.

How am I going to get everything done before the first day of school? Now that I finally have the names of my students, I need to assign textbooks, set up my grade book, and create seating charts. I haven't duplicated handouts and gathered supplies for the first week of school. We were cutting it close.

These experienced teachers had worked together for many years, and the questions they asked reflected that, such as if procedures for tutoring kids after school would remain the same and is such-and-such kid still receiving medical treatment for this or that condition. Of course, I hadn't a clue what they were talking about.

Mrs. G was a teacher in the lower school, and her son, Wayne, was in Mrs. A's sixth grade homeroom and English class. He had diabetes, so she gave everyone a brief lecture on how to handle if he had an episode. I was glad he wasn't in my class because I freeze in an emergency. If somebody is standing in front of me bleeding profusely, I watch the blood pool on the floor.

One day before Christmas, Wayne was in my class for a special holiday activity, and he had an episode where his blood sugar dropped and he came close to passing out. He sat in his seat with his eyes closed and his head on the desk.

He uttered, "I don't feel good."

19

"Ms. B," one of his classmates called. "Wayne needs help. It's an emergency!"

My mouth dropped open, and I stood there looking at Wayne.

"Ummmm...," I uttered.

"We have to do something," another child said.

"Tracy, run across the hall and get Mrs. A," I directed. *I'm doing good*, I thought. *I did something.*

Fortunately, she came right away prepared. She brought a package of cookies and gave him one. Then she directed someone to get him a drink of water. He perked up, so she had a student walk him to the nurse's office. A disaster had been averted and he was okay. Thank goodness!

I didn't know the non-middle school teachers very well, but I had learned their names. Some had introduced themselves. Others seemed to shy away from me. I was too busy to give it any thought. I figured they were not open to receiving newcomers.

Whenever I didn't know something, Mrs. A was my "go-to" person. I sat next to her in case I had any questions. I didn't want to raise my hand and ask something trivial or foolish in front of the whole faculty.

I went to Mrs. A when I wanted to run a bulletin board idea past her. I walked into her room and saw one of the most amazing bulletin boards I had ever seen in my life. I hadn't realized she was so talented. She had stapled indoor/outdoor carpet to the board and made a soccer field with lines and players. Her slogan was "Score High in English." As students received points for participation and good behavior, she advanced the soccer ball on the field.

They would earn a party or some kind of reward if they scored a goal.

When I marveled at the board and asked her what she thought of my idea, she said, "I never save old bulletin boards, otherwise I'd lend you something of mine."

I didn't ask you that, but okay….

She was standing in her closet, and she pointed to a few empty shelves. I thought it a nice sentiment, but I didn't need any supplies. I presumed she didn't like my bulletin board idea, although I put it up anyway and other teachers and students complimented it. I hung orange paper and placed enticing young adult book jackets in a large Halloween cobweb I stapled to the paper. The slogan was "Get Caught Up in Reading."

After I resigned at the end of the following year (Yes, I stayed two years!!!), I returned to pick up my supplies and found Mrs. A's soccer bulletin board hanging in my former classroom. She had given it to my replacement who, the school secretary informed me, was Catholic and now chummy with my former teaching partner. Mrs. A must have stored her supplies at home. I wasn't surprised. In addition, I couldn't find the supplies for which I had returned, so I assumed Mrs. A had thrown them away. I could envision her tossing my belongings into the trash, happy to get rid of anything that reminded her of me.

I was happy with my schedule, as it was relatively straightforward. I liked the double class periods because we had a lot to cover in English Language Arts. (We were required to give each student separate grades for vocabulary, literature and grammar.) Each class period was 90 minutes instead of the usual 45 minutes, which meant we could accomplish much more in one class period.

I had my sixth grade class first and second periods, then my seventh grade third and fourth periods, and the eighth graders I would see after lunch at the end of the day. I had a planning period for 45 minutes after lunch before the eighth graders.

That wasn't much time to accomplish everything that needed to be done, such as writing lesson and unit plans, gathering and creating materials, making phone calls to parents, grading papers or tests, and at certain times completing interim reports or report cards. I would take work home every night and work after dinner until bedtime. I also worked on Sundays. I would allow myself Saturdays off to make sure I didn't burn out. Besides, my father would remind me that Saturdays were our Sabbath which is a day of rest. On Saturday nights I would go out with friends or, on occasion, a date. When the school year started, I didn't have a boyfriend.

The faculty meeting concluded, and I was packing my belongings when I heard someone mention moving elsewhere.

"What?" I asked. "Where are we going?"

"To church," responded the social studies teacher.

What? Church?!

Seeing my look of disbelief, she continued, "We do this every year before school starts. This is just for the teachers."

Church??? I have to go to church??? I'll pass on this.

As if she read my mind, she said, "Everyone is required to go. Come on."

22

I'm required to go to church? How could they force me to go? Was this in my contract? Didn't they all know I was Jewish?

I was never one to be contrary, so I went along. Besides, I didn't know how to get out of it. The principal would notice I was missing.

I had no idea where the church was located, so I followed everyone. I dragged my feet down the hallway feeling "like a lamb to the slaughter." I may as well have been shackled as reluctant as I was to go. I had no idea what to expect.

The church wasn't far. We walked to the end of the corridor and around the corner. There, another smaller corridor led to a light-filled atrium. I had heard this extension and new construction was recent, and it showed by its magnitude alone. The wide open space was lined with windowed walls and decorated with tall white pillars and fresh, new flooring. The wooden doors to the church looked like the entrance to a medieval castle. They opened to a space so big that NASA could have built a rocket ship in there.

A round stone baptismal was inside. I knew what it was from movies and television, yet I'd never seen one in person. A metal bowl trickled water into the pool. I thought this would be lovely if it were a fountain. At Christmas time they surrounded it with red poinsettias.

The inside of the church was hexagon-shaped and had seating for at least a couple thousand worshippers. Overhead was a twenty-four foot high vaulted ceiling with beautiful exposed wooden beams that matched the long, polished pews. The pipe organs set high above the altar were gleaming silver. Each pew had a moveable bar underneath.

I would find out later it was a knee rest for kneeling. There was a wooden cross hanging above the altar so big it would have held a giant-sized Jesus! I knew not all churches were this massive.

How did they get a church this nice? This must cost a fortune!

I tried to stay toward the back of the group so I'd be seated in the second row. But I miscalculated and ended up in the first row because the pews held so many people. Our group filled the pews at the front of the sanctuary. Behind us were rows and rows of empty pews. It reminded me of a funeral service where the dearly departed had no one who came to mourn.

I sat uncomfortably, squeezed between teachers, my hands folded in my lap. I looked around at the big, open church. I had been in a church before but never during a service. What would they ask me to do? I wished that I were a church mouse, and I could scramble through a hole and disappear. It didn't feel like one person sensed or cared how uneasy I felt. We sat so closely together someone should have sensed the heat emanating from my body, my legs shaking slightly, or my arms twitching.

I was accustomed to religious services, because I had attended many synagogue services. Although in my synagogue, each attendee has his or her own seat, the hinged kind that flips up when you stand. When I was a youngster, I was so lightweight that, like the jaws of a crocodile, the seat snapped closed and folded me up in it!

My mother was a reform Jew and not observant. The only time she went to synagogue was once a year during

Yom Kippur to say Yizkor, a memorial prayer, for her parents. Ironically, Yizkor is said four times a year.

My father, on the other hand, considered himself an Orthodox Jew who kept the Sabbath and holidays. He often went to services and many times would take me with him.

In a synagogue there is a bema similar to an altar, and the religious leader is a rabbi. In Jewish orthodox services the men and women sit separately, and the women do not stand on the bema to read Torah, the holy scripture. Additionally, most of the service is in Hebrew which I learned how to read in Sunday/Hebrew school.

I ended up a Conservative Jew which is somewhere in the middle. I am comfortable sitting with men and women during a service. I noticed that the church had prayer books as we do in synagogue. While there was no Torah, there were objects displayed that looked to have religious significance. I did attend a service once at a reform Jewish temple that used an organ. I was accustomed, though, to no musical accompaniment, so I startled when I heard the symphonic melody of the pipe organ that reminded me of the overture to *Phantom of the Opera*.

The pastor started speaking. His booming voice bounced off the high ceilings and empty pews. He welcomed us and recited prayers. The teachers recited along with him. I sat silently.

Whew; it's just a service.

At least this service was in English. But, as one would expect, there were lots of mentions of Jesus Christ. That was difficult for me. You would never hear His name come from my father's lips. Nor would he ever write it. If he had to write "Christmas," he'd write it as "x-mas." As a matter of fact, when we'd drive past a local church, my father would say, "Our rabbi told me that Jews should never go into a church." Ironically, here I sat.

Sorry, Dad. How many of your rules have I already broken just by working here?

My father grew up in an Orthodox Jewish household in Baltimore City, the son of immigrants who fled Poland and Russia in the early 1900's due to persecution of the Jews. Both my parents had relatives who perished in the Holocaust. Both had grown up with childhood incidents of being taunted and beaten due to their religion.

They sent me to a public elementary school where I was the minority among a population of African Americans. I was friendly with everyone. To my knowledge, no one ever mentioned my religion or ridiculed me about it. While my parents were sensitive to these issues, they made sure I led a relatively protected life.

When I learned of the Holocaust in Hebrew School, I had a nightmare that the Nazis were invading our home. I have never forgotten the scene that played out in my sleep—the soldiers entering my bedroom and pulling me out of bed with their guns pointed. I was standing before them in my long pink nightgown, trembling, about to urinate on my lime green bedroom carpet, unsure of what torture they were going to use on me. The nightmare has always served as a reminder of my ancestry.

The fact that I was teaching at a Catholic school upset my father. He wasn't thrilled about the Virgin Mary lodged in my classroom whom he saw when he helped me bring my materials to school. But he had resigned himself to letting me "do my thing," even though, every so often, he tried to talk me out of teaching there.

"You know you can leave anytime," he'd say to me occasionally.

"Are you sure you haven't changed your mind about teaching there?" he'd ask.

My mother didn't seem bothered by it.

I knew not to kneel in church as that would be considered bowing before Jesus Christ. I must have learned that in Hebrew School. I had no interest in taking communion. And if anybody thought I was going to cross myself, they were crazy!

If my father knew I was here, he'd pitch a fit. I will never tell him that I am going to church services. He'd make me quit my job immediately.

I sat listening, enjoying a hymn, and admiring the splendor of this newly created, magnificent House of Worship. I started to relax a little and feel a little less out of place.

Then the pastor announced, "I invite you all to come up and join me." His arms were outstretched, and the sleeves of his long white robe cascaded to the floor. He reminded me of an albatross about to take flight.

You want us to do what? Come up there?

All the teachers stepped up to the altar, while I remained seated. The two eighth grade homeroom teachers waved me up, encouraging me to join them. I politely nodded my head "no." But they wouldn't give up. So begrudgingly, I dragged myself up there. After all, I wasn't a rabble-rouser.

"Let us all hold hands," the pastor instructed. My hands were grabbed from each side.

There's no running away now! At least they aren't holding my hands behind my back and forcing me to bow down. How many times throughout history were the Jews forced to bow down to other gods?

At least their grip isn't iron tight, so I could still run away if I had to.

What now? I assume we aren't going to do a folk dance. I hope I won't be asked to speak. Please don't put me on the spot and ask me to recite some prayer I don't know.

Are we going to turn out the lights and use candles? Are we going to perform some kind of ritualistic ceremony? Is there a lamb to be slaughtered or some kind of sacrifice to make? It isn't me, is it?! Are they going to ask me to chant something in Latin? What have I gotten myself into?

The leader directed us to bow our heads. After watching everyone else, I did the same.

"Let us pray," he said. "We pray for a good school year. We pray that our students will learn and grow with us."

My whole body relaxed and I started breathing again. I felt the grip of the teachers' hands.

Did they notice my hands are sweaty?

The leader continued, "We pray that we make the best possible decisions for our students."

He prayed a little more and asked the Lord to watch over us. When he stopped speaking, everyone dropped hands.

That was a beautiful prayer, and one I agree with wholeheartedly. You don't have to be Christian to deliver a prayer like that.

As my body started to relax, I could feel my toes again in my dress shoes.

I have to stop getting so worked up. It's only a prayer. They didn't even mention Jesus Christ this time.

During my interview the principal had informed me that I was required to bring the children to services. I didn't realize the frequency, once a month or more. The first time I took my homeroom class to church, I directed them to sit in the pews. After they filed in, I turned to head out the door when I noticed all the teachers seated with their classes.

Oh no! Am I supposed to stay? Nobody told me that. I wonder if they would say anything if I just walked out. There's the door. It's only about fifteen feet away. I could just walk out as if I have somewhere to be. I better not. If I do that, I'll probably get in trouble.

I sat down next to the last student.

Darn it. I know I'm expected to be here. They seem to always expect these things of me.

I asked Mrs. A after we returned to our classes and I saw her in the hallway. She confirmed that I was required to stay. I grew accustomed to attending church services, even learning several prayers. By the end of the year I told some friends that I felt as though I was half Jewish and half Catholic! I was actually proud that I was familiar with a religion other than my own.

When the teachers' service was over, I was happy we were permitted to go home early. I couldn't wait to get out of there! I'd already been forced to do something that didn't feel right. I thought I should have been given the option of my level of participation since everyone knew I am Jewish. A little warning beforehand would have been appreciated as well!

Chapter 3

Thy Kingdom Come

After my welcome note had been taken away on that first day, I had no time to dwell on it. I put it out of my mind and focused on the students who would be arriving within the hour. I had a long day ahead with lots of work to do. I was excited to meet my students, but at the same time, there were random butterflies doing figure eights in my stomach. I expected that I would experience this, but once the children joined me, the butterflies landed, and I felt enveloped by a warm cocoon and the sanctuary we created together. Being with them made me happy.

The first bell rang, and since I couldn't see the front of the school, I could only imagine the throng of children pushing their way through the doors. Several moments later there was the turbulence and cacophony of a herd in the distance. Then, like cattle who couldn't be wrangled, an offshoot headed down the hallway, a mixture of third through eighth graders. Students of various sizes donned in plaid and navy school uniforms with backpacks and lunch bags were "looming large on the horizon."

Mrs. A reappeared right after the bell rang to inform me that all the teachers have hall duty every day and are required to stand in the hallway between classes to monitor students. That was news to me. It was a good thing my classroom was ready since I wasn't going back inside until the students arrived.

I have to stand in the hallway every day? There goes more of my valuable time. Can't they find other people to monitor the hallways? Was this in my job description?

We both stood lookout by our doors. The sixth grade homeroom students knew which classroom was theirs since most of them were next door in fifth grade the previous year. Plus, they knew if they had Mrs. A or "the other teacher." I greeted my students with a pleasant "Good Morning" that would become my daily routine. They brushed past me into my classroom, mumbling something unintelligible, not very concerned with the new teacher but more annoyed by the early hour, the lack of sleep and the end of a slower summertime pace. As I greeted each student, I kept my other eye on the incoming traffic to make sure there were no jams, collisions or road rage. Since the hallways had no lockers, it was an easier job than in public school.

As the children entered, I instructed them to sit anywhere for the time being. I had arranged the desks in a more modern way than they were accustomed. While my teaching partner had the traditional layout with all the desks facing forward toward hers, I chose to arrange the desks around the perimeter of the room, facing inward, two rows deep forming three sides of a rectangle. The front of the rectangle I left open, and I could easily walk over to anyone. It allowed open space that I planned to use if we were going to act something out or needed floor space for a project or assignment.

Mrs. A. had appeared in my classroom the day I had rearranged the desks.

"What's this?" she asked.

"I'm trying a new seating arrangement. I think I like it. It's a little different and leaves space for students to sit on the floor when we do an activity."

"Well, we'll see how that works," she snarled, turning on her heels and walking out.

I guess she doesn't like it.

The arrangement worked so well that I never changed it. The students enjoyed sitting on the floor when working on group book projects and other assignments. Even the DARE officer (police officer who comes to teach the kids to "say no to drugs") commented how much he liked the arrangement, especially when he had them act out skits.

While the school seemed to be a mixture of old and new, the actual seats for the students were "vintage." I imagined that students who attended this school in the 1950s used the same desks. They were the old wooden chairs with the desktops attached and space underneath for books. You often see the more modern version of plastic, fiberboard and chrome today on college campuses or in places where space is limited.

On this first day, a larger seventh grade girl muttered, "Oh dear," as she wedged her wide bottom into the narrow seat opening. She must have been accustomed to this, because she withstood the obvious discomfort without complaint, and thankfully no one teased her. I asked her later in private if she'd like me to find her a different type of seat, and she said "No, thank you." I thought that her manners and the politeness of her classmates spoke well of the school.

I guess she doesn't mind cramming herself into this seat every day. I would have jumped at the opportunity to sit in something else. I guess she doesn't want to call attention to herself. She's right. That would make her stand out, and I can't think of another solution. I'm sure they won't let me change all the desks in my room.

"Ms. B, I'm a lefty not a righty," Billy asserted.

"Oh.....Just do the best you can for now," was all I had to offer.

"I'll try to find out if they make these seats with the desk on the other side," I remarked at the end of the class period after I had watched him contort his whole body like Houdini to be able to fill out a form. I never found one after asking just about everybody in the school, including the maintenance worker.

How can they not have one lefty desk in this whole building? They obviously don't care about students with differences.

The next day I suggested that my lefty student put an empty desk adjacent to his and use that surface for writing instead. He declined that offer.

I presumed my students would be the most well-behaved students since this was a Catholic school, and they were required to wear uniforms, attend religion class and church services, and adhere to strict rules I heard about in the faculty meetings. For example, I was told to assign homework every night. I didn't agree with this, because that's a lot of homework accrued for one night from every teacher. Plus, my lessons didn't always require work to be done for the next day, nor did the students need to do work every night to reinforce the learning that took place. And sometimes they just deserved a break!

I was also told to be strict, and that if a child came to class without a writing instrument, he or she was to receive a detention on the spot. I didn't agree with that either. As a matter of fact, several months into the school year I had a student come to class for an entire week without a pen or pencil. When I finally gave him a detention and asked him the next day for the consent form signed by a parent, he said, "My parents told me to tell you I'm not going to serve it."

"Why not, Joseph?"

"That's what they said."

I called his home and left several messages for his parents who never called me back. I trudged outside to the parking lot during dismissal, risking life and limb to find his mother amid the stampede of students making their end-of-the-day, I-can't-wait-to-go-home escape.

I shouted her name, but she didn't answer.

I ran up to her and tapped her on the shoulder.

"Excuse me, but you know your son got a detention from me, right?"

"Yes, I know."

"I know?" You have nothing else to say?

"Well, he didn't return the consent form. He can't serve it without that. Did you sign it?"

"You'll have to talk to my husband."

34

"Can't you sign the consent form? He needs to serve this detention."

"I'm not going to speak to you about this. You'll have to talk to my husband." She walked away.

What?! What's with that? She acts like I did something wrong. Why can't she address this issue? This is pretty "cut and dry." It's not like this is something disputable. The kid came to English class repeatedly without something to write with. It's the policy of this school to receive a detention for that. I was even nice about it, and let him get away with it for days. Why won't she answer me?

I never found out what the story was, but later I assumed it was yet another parent who didn't approve of me teaching in the school and was giving me a hard time. When I sought the advice of other middle school teachers, they told me to "let it go."

Did they know something they weren't telling me?

After a number of students had gathered in the room on this first day, I peeked in to find average eleven and twelve-year-olds greeting each other after time away and chatting about summer vacations. I forgot most of them were familiar with each other after attending school here since kindergarten. This wasn't usually the case in public school. Some of them were so tall, they could have been eighth graders. And some of them looked like they still belonged in elementary school.

Oh, they gave me some babies, I thought. *I'll take good care of them.*

After the frenzy in the hallway died down, and it appeared that all my students were present, I entered my classroom and shut the door. I was about to address my homeroom class when the loud speaker crackled and a voice announcing the start of school broadcast into the room. Nobody seemed to notice my slight jolt, and I shut my mouth. I was so eager to start that I had forgotten about the morning announcements!

I froze in place and listened with the students. After a few words, everyone stood for the Pledge of Allegiance. I placed my hand over my heart and recited the words along with the students. I was checking around the room to ensure that everyone was reciting it and scoping out any troublemakers that weren't. So far I had a group of good American citizens.

Next, the recitation of the Lord's Prayer began. The children automatically bowed their heads.

Why hadn't I foreseen this? I thought. *Hadn't I learned my lesson yet? Didn't I think there would be prayers?*

The Virgin Mary already had her head bowed not far from the loudspeaker. In order to be respectful, I bowed my head also, but I did not utter the words. I raised my head once to check that all the students were reciting the prayer. It appeared that these students were very respectful or very well-trained. After the Lord's Prayer everyone seated themselves automatically with military precision. There was no need for any direction from me.

So glad I don't need to say anything!

Finally, I walked to the front of the room and introduced myself, welcomed the kids, and took attendance. I tried right away to learn the names of the twenty-five students in my homeroom class. We were discussing their class schedules, and I was trying to ensure that everyone was familiar with where they were going when the bell rang. Some of the students stayed with me for English Language Arts while others moved directly across the hall to Mrs. A. I was glad that I had some of her students in my homeroom so that I could get to know other sixth graders.

After the brief shuffle, I looked around at the different faces. I had directed the "new" students to also sit anywhere until I moved them to assigned seats which I did speedily after I introduced myself again.

I took a deep breath, as this seemed like a very ordinary first day of school. I suppose I hadn't known what to expect after receiving my "love note." No hands flew up accusing me of being a Jew and asking why I was in the school. So far so good!

I distributed copies of "Ms. B's Classroom Rules, Regulations and Policies" and went over each item, trying to sound like a cross between a drill sergeant and a nun. It's always important for a teacher to lay the ground work right away so students know your expectations, what you consider proper conduct and what your procedures are for managing your classroom. In other words, this is to stop bad behavior before it starts. They can't use the excuse that they didn't know. If anyone considers misbehaving this early on, this will give them pause, at least temporarily. Even on the first day of school, it is usually easy to identify the more challenging students, especially if they call any of the rules into question.

With my rules, regulations and policies, I tried to be concise and specific. I was conveying to my students that I expected appropriate and orderly behavior and for students to come to class prepared and organized. But I also expected them to enjoy themselves, learn a lot and even have fun, which I made sure to tell them.

Then I had my administrative duties to perform with forms to complete, textbooks to assign, and dress code and fire procedures to review.

Time flew, and before I knew it, they were out the door, and my seventh graders sat before me. I felt confident and happy. One class down and two more to go. I liked the kids. I think that in all my teaching days there was never a kid I disliked no matter how he or she behaved, as I got to know each and every one of them quite well.

It was the same procedure with my seventh grade class. It isn't difficult to tell the difference between sixth and seventh graders. Sixth graders appear less mature and developed. A lot of physical growth happens over the summer so that seventh graders are usually taller. They gain more confidence and have a more developed sense of humor (sometimes to the point of being mouthy).

Seventh graders ask all sorts of questions. I had to tell them to wait until I was finished reading through the rules before I would take questions. They asked good questions, mostly about tests and quizzes and my grading policy which was not specifically mentioned on the handout.

Once they left, I could finally go to the rest room. During my teaching experience, I became an expert at holding my bladder for long periods of time. While some people might brag about awards or commendations, I boasted about how many hours I could go without a bathroom break.

I was glad it was lunchtime. I was starving! I barely had anything to eat before school started. I didn't want to go to lunch alone, so I walked across the hall to ask Mrs. A if she was going. I found her sitting at her desk with an unwrapped sandwich placed neatly in front of her. She was chewing a bite when I walked in.

"Are you going to lunch?" I asked her anyway.

"I meat in my massroom," she said with a mouthful. She didn't even swallow before she answered me.

I guess I won't be eating lunch with her this year. I don't know anybody else I'd want to eat with. What am I going to do?

I had packed my lunch since I was unsure where the cafeteria was, what food was available, and if there was enough time to buy lunch.

So I begrudgingly walked back up the steps, down the long corridor, and into the faculty room on the corner. I stopped and took a look around. It was a cramped little room with round tables. There were a handful of teachers in the room, but none of the middle school teachers. Nobody invited me to sit at their table. I took a deep breath and sat by myself. I could hear the chatter of the other teachers but their talk was about the younger students. Except for the foreign language teacher who asked how my first day was going, nobody spoke to me. I was a little puzzled, as I thought more people would have asked or at least said hello.

I went directly back to my classroom after lunch and used my planning period to straighten up, review my seating charts and students' names, write notes on my lessons from today and prepare for tomorrow. Forty five minutes goes by fast.

I had met a few of my eighth grade students before the school year started, since they had visited during teacher preparation week.

I was out in the hallway hanging a sign on my door when I noticed a group of kids closer to the lobby greeting teachers. I could hear exclamations from the teachers, and I saw them go out in the hallway and hug the students.

What well-liked students. Or it's just such a small school that everyone is very familiar with each other.

These students were slowly making their way down the hallway. I knew it was only a matter of time before they visited my classroom.

Sure enough, about fifteen minutes later there were four adolescents invading my room. They didn't wait for an invitation but seated themselves on the back ledge by the windows.

Look how comfortable they are. They seem very familiar with the school.

From across the room they told me their names and asked mine and what I was doing.

I stopped the paperwork at my desk and walked over to answer their questions.

"Are you our new teacher?" one of them asked.

"I was waiting for you to ask me that," I replied, smiling. "Indeed, I am."

They pointed out the two that would be in my class and told me whose classes they had last year. They were talkative and full of youthful enthusiasm, telling me what they did over summer vacation and what high school they wanted to go to. I was impressed that they made this effort to meet me.

It was the first day of school and here they were as formal students. It was 1:30 PM and time for my last class. Even though I knew ahead of time this was a much smaller class with only twelve kids, the reality hit me when they were all seated and most of the seats were empty. I thought that having a small group would be a real pleasure and a relaxing ending to the day, but I was wrong. It wasn't going to be so easy. A number of these kids were full of personality and energy and would prove to be more challenging.

It didn't take them long to start asking me questions.

"How old are you? Where did you go to college? Are you married? Do you have any children? Do you have a boyfriend? Have you ever taught before? Is your hair naturally curly?"

It's a good thing I'm not a beginner teacher.

Among these vibrant personalities were a few students so quiet that I wondered if they could speak. I would attempt to "draw them out" throughout the school year. The other students more than made up for their silence.

Unlike my other classes, I let these students choose seats the first day. This was a fatal mistake. After Day One, it became difficult to get the talkers to be quiet. I moved them around and put them in every other seat to create some distance between them.

Since this class was small, we could move through material more quickly. After we completed the administrative minutia, we started an actual lesson.

Wow. I'll have to remember to plan a lot more for this class. This is exciting that we actually get to do some real work today!

Their first assignment was to write a brief autobiography which would serve not only as a way for me to learn about them but also as a diagnostic tool to assess their current level of writing. This composition assignment would take several days to complete. We started with an interest inventory that I had pulled from my stored teaching materials. (An interest inventory is a questionnaire about likes and dislikes). Then students wrote a first draft. I always completed my assignments along with the students and often shared my writing. That was the case with this assignment as well.

Being outspoken students in an open atmosphere I tried to foster, the students freely made suggestions. One student, Greg, suggested they read each other's completed papers and guess who's who.

What a great idea! These kids are going to keep me on my toes! It's not often that a student has a good suggestion for how to do a lesson!

I used his suggestion, and the students enjoyed it. I also learned miscellaneous information, such as Greg had a sister in the fifth grade; Peter had a twin brother in Mrs. A's class, his younger sister was in my seventh grade class and his older siblings had all attended this school; and Talia's mother teaches at this school in a lower grade.

Showing their inquisitive nature, they asked to hear my autobiography, so I shared. I started with my name. Then I read, "I was named after my grandfather, David. Therefore, my Hebrew name (I am Jewish) is the female version of the name David." I said where I went to college and my previous work experience. I read, "I welcome all my students this year and look forward to a fabulous school year where my students and I will accomplish many goals and enjoy the learning experiences we will share together." I looked up at the kids.

"You're Jewish?!" Colin asked without raising his hand. Most of the students looked astounded.

"Yes, I am," I answered. "Please raise your hand next time."

"Are you allowed to teach here?" Mary Ann asked without raising her hand. How quickly my rules, regulations and policies seemed to fly out the window.

"Yes," I answered. "Please raise your hand in class."

"How is it that you are allowed to teach here?" Douglas asked, raising his hand as he asked the question.

I remained silent until he raised his hand and waited for me to address him. He repeated the question.

"Well, I'm teaching you English Language Arts," I explained. "That shouldn't interfere with anything else."

I was glad to see that Jennifer raised her hand and waited for me to call on her.

"Do you have horns?" she asked sincerely.

"Do I have what?"

"Horns. I heard that Jewish people have horns on their heads."

"No, I don't have horns. Jewish people do not have horns. Although sometimes my curls do stick straight up," I said pulling on a curl. That got a little laugh.

Oh my G-d! I can't believe she just asked me that! They really think that? How can they believe that? What have they been told and by whom? I heard people believed that, but I thought that was a long time ago.

Colin waited to be called on.

"Yes?"

"Can we ask you about your religion?"

"Of course you can. You can ask me whatever you like. I'd be happy to answer any questions if I actually know the answer. But not if it takes away from a lot of class time. And it's time to get ready for dismissal."

I wondered if these kids were ever exposed to people of other religions. It reminded me of when I discovered a close elementary school friend was a Jehovah's Witness. One day when we were playing on my parents' patio, I asked her questions about it. She was answering me when my mother interrupted. She must have been listening.

"Diane, come in this house this instant," she instructed. "Lisa, we'll see you later." She slammed the door shut.

"Stop listening to her. You shouldn't be listening to her talk about her religion."

"But, mom, I asked her about it. She was only answering me."

"I don't want to hear it. You shouldn't be learning about any other religion."

"But, mom, I was interested. I want to find out what it's about."

"If you don't follow my directions, you won't be allowed to play with her anymore."

"Okay, mom," I acquiesced.

To this day I believe my parents overreacted. It would have been educational for me to learn about her religion.

44

I also think my parents had received a lot of door-to-door solicitors trying to convert people to Jehovah's Witnesses, so they were wary. Lisa and her family were not one of them though. I didn't want anyone at this school to think I was soliciting either. I knew I had to be careful.

All in all, I was pleased with how the first day had gone. My butterflies had flown away and wouldn't reappear for the remainder of the school year. However, I was emotionally and physically exhausted and couldn't wait to get home. The welcome note had already disappeared from my mind.

Chapter 4

Thy Will be Done

In the public school system, I had been given a curriculum guide to help me teach. This guide, created mostly by teachers, was a huge help in lesson planning. In addition to providing specific units, within each unit were objectives, suggestions for activities, and handouts that could be used directly with the students. Private schools rarely give teachers curriculum guides.

Today "Common Core" has standardized teaching objectives throughout the nation in the hopes that all students will meet the same expectations at the same points throughout their learning and be ready and prepared for higher learning and the work force. This was developed over many years with the help of teachers. "Common Core" has, in a sense, revolutionized teaching methods in that they dictate more of how teachers should introduce concepts, explain them and help the students learn the material.

Instead, at this school I had been given a list of objectives with sets of literature and grammar textbooks. It was like being given a recipe without the directions. You know what you want to make and you have the ingredients, but the steps are missing. Teachers must figure out the details themselves. Each daily lesson plan has a structure with different parts, and the teacher must create them, deciding which activities to do and how long they will take. She also needs to address different learning styles and needs of the students and include different methods of interaction in the classroom, such as group work or students working in pairs. I tried to be creative with how I handled the course content, and I always tried to make my lessons enjoyable.

Our first unit was "The Story and Its Elements" which I used with all three grades but with modifications for each. For the eighth grade, I used more difficult stories and activities. I chose this unit because the content was covered at the beginning of the literature books since it included the fundamental elements of literature. In addition, I had taught something similar in my student teaching and long-term substitute experiences. While this is primarily a literature unit about plot, conflict, setting, characters and theme, since I was teaching integrated Language Arts, I wove vocabulary, grammar, and composition into it.

One of the activities I included was to have the students do improvisation, acting out fictitious situations I created. This kept them actively engaged and stressed the importance of character, plot, and setting. One scenario was that an elephant has escaped from the zoo and is found in someone's backyard. In my seventh grade class, Billy took the lead in this one. He was a light-skinned Caucasian boy with freckles and light brown hair who reminded me of Opie from the Andy Griffith show. Looking out our back window with his mouth agape and his eyes wide, he feigned shock and disbelief that grazing behind our classroom was a ten-ton tusked, gray, African mammoth.

"Holy cow, how did that get out there?" he exclaimed, pointing to the lawn behind us.

"That's not a cow; that's an elephant!" a second boy proclaimed.

"How are we going to get it out of here?" Billy asked. "We need to return it to the zoo."

"We need to put it to sleep," a third boy directed, passing out imaginary tranquilizer guns.

Aiming at the elephant who, by this time, had magically appeared in our room, bypassing any normal entry points, the boys pulled their triggers, and supposedly the elephant fell to the ground, although none of us felt the proverbial earth shake.

"Did it work?" they asked each other, bending down to examine the body.

"Yes, I think he's asleep," the third boy answered.

"Let's get him out of here," Billy directed.

Spreading themselves around the large open area of the room, they each pretended to lift a part of the unconscious elephant. They heaved, pulled, and moaned for several minutes, feigning exhaustion, stopping to sit down, asking for water, and then eventually pretending to drag the massive, hefty carcass out the door, which somehow magically fit through the narrow opening. That was one of several noteworthy performances, and afterward we had a nice discussion about the elements of narration. All the students had a great time and asked me to include more activities of this nature in the future.

Later in the school year we travelled to the younger grades to perform scenes and one-act plays. Some students performed original works like a fractured (also known as twisted) fairy tale, a fairy tale where the plot, characters, setting, or some other element has changed. I knew the younger kids were excited, because their teachers told me how they were counting down the days until our arrival. They could barely stay in their seats when they saw us. They were clapping and cheering before anything started. My students felt like movie stars.

One of the most memorable performances was by a group of my seventh graders who chose to reenact the main chocolate room scene from Roald Dahl's *Willie Wonka and the Chocolate Factory*. We had made a chocolate river from a long roll of brown bulletin board paper, and they couldn't have picked a more fitting actor to play Augustus Gloop. Franco was a short, rotund, brown-skinned boy who liked to "ham it up." His black hair was in a bowl cut with straight bangs like Moe from the Three Stooges. For his part, he knelt down by the river and pretended to slurp up the chocolate with his hands.

He delivered his lines with his prepubescent high-pitched enthusiastic voice, "Mmmmm....this stuff is *terr-rifffiiccc*. I need a bucket to drink it properly."

As he put his hands to his face, he secretly smeared chocolate hidden in his fists. I wish I had a photograph of his clown-like appearance with his round face, chubby cheeks and full lips all smothered in melted chocolate. We were all hysterical.

Then he pretended to fall into the river, rolling and thrashing about on the paper as he screamed, "Help! Help! I can't swim!"

To add to the frolic and histrionics, four students dressed as oompa loompas, the short chocolate workers in Wonka's factory. They wore white t-shirts with big O's on the front, but skipped face paint and wigs. With arms crossed and deep knee bends, they sang the song from the original 1971 soundtrack:

Oompa loompa doompety doo

I've got a perfect puzzle for you

Oompa loompa doompety dee

If you are wise you'll listen to me

What do you get when you guzzle down sweets

Eating as much as an elephant eats

What are you at, getting terribly fat

What do you think will come of that

I don't like the look of it

Oompa loompa doompety da

If you're not greedy, you will go far

You will live in happiness too

Like the Oompa Loompa Doompety do

Doompety do

— Anthony Newley / Leslie Bricusse

My students were thrilled to receive thank-you notes from the young audience members. They couldn't wait for another opportunity to perform. The other half of the sixth, seventh and eighth graders heard what great performances my students gave and requested performances too.

So we honored their requests, continued our "road show," and visited the middle school classrooms as well.

Starting from the beginning of the year, we would often read together in class, initially with short stories but eventually advancing to novels. I gave students time every week to read a book of their choice in class. Each child had a journal, which was a marble composition book, that we used to write reader's responses. We reviewed what makes a good journal entry and examined different types. I kept a list hanging on the wall. Some of the items on the list were to summarize a chapter, write about how they relate to an incident or character, write a letter to a friend or teacher about something they read, make a prediction, write a poem or song about something in the book, or write something else if they were inspired. Sometimes I would pair them to share journal entries. I would often pair myself with a willing student. From time to time I would take the journals home (one class at a time but still a heavy load) and respond to their entries. I enjoyed reading them.

The children were welcome to bring their own books or library books to class to read. I checked to make sure the books were appropriate and on grade level.

Mrs. A popped her head in my room one day during my planning period.

"Diane, Mr. Z needs to see you right away. He's waiting for you. Go now and don't waste any time," she said ominously. She ducked out.

What did I do? Why on earth am I being summoned to the principal's office? Why does it sound so urgent? Does Mrs. A know what he wants and doesn't want to tell me? What am I in trouble for?

51

I dropped what I was doing and headed down the corridor, shuffling my feet on the carpet like a shackled prisoner making the long walk to the execution chair. I'm surprised I didn't electrocute myself with all the static electricity I generated. With each step I could hear the figurative chains rattle as I wracked my brain trying to figure out what I could possibly have done wrong. I hadn't had a conversation with Mr. Z since my interview. I couldn't think of one reason why he would ask to see me. Did I say something wrong to a student or a teacher? Did I neglect to turn in some important piece of paperwork? Is he ripping up my contract and firing me on the spot? Maybe I was just being paranoid, and he actually wanted to compliment me for something.

I stood squeamishly in front of his door, took a deep breath and forced myself to knock. I considered running back to my classroom, but I didn't think that was a good idea.

"Come in," I heard through the door. I opened the door and took a few steps inside. He didn't offer me a seat or shake my hand. He got right to the point.

"There was a group of your sixth graders who came to see me," he said.

Oh my gosh! Whaaaat??!

"And their parents have complained as well."

Holy crap! I really must have done something wrong! What were they complaining about?

I tried to remain composed, but once again I was sweating in his office even though the temperature was just right. *Was I getting fired after only working a few weeks? What did I do?*

What would happen to my students if they replaced me? I don't want to leave.

"You have no library in your room. The kids want to have books."

"What?"

"Books," he answered a little louder. "The kids want books. They want to be able to select their own books to read for leisure."

"They do select their own books for leisure," I replied.

"They want to be able to select books from your classroom."

Well, that's great!" I exclaimed.

"You need a classroom library."

"We have a school library. I was going to take them as a class next week so they could check out books. I've already made arrangements."

"They are accustomed to the teacher having a shelf with books on it for them. They don't want to have to go to the library," he said, sighing exasperatedly.

"Oh," I responded. "Our own library?"

"Yes," he answered impatiently through clenched teeth. He was obviously perturbed, and so was I, as our conversation seemed to be going in circles. I felt like the village idiot.

"Well, I think it's great that they want a classroom library. I would love to have one. But it'll take some time to put together."

This is why I've been called to the office? This is my major offense? It's only the second week of school and my first full year of teaching, and they are upset because I don't have a book collection? And why are they bringing this to the principal's attention and not to me?

53

"We can provide you with a bookshelf," he said.

"Okay...." I paused for a moment. "I would hope that my students would feel comfortable enough to come to me and tell me this themselves."

"I'll have someone bring you a bookshelf when we find one," he responded. "Thanks."

I left his office and returned to my classroom, puzzled by this whole affair. I would have to "feel out" my sixth graders and try to find out what was going on. Now I had to focus on how to get books for my classroom. Of course the school didn't offer to pay for them. It was expected that I would use my own money, as I did for all my bulletin board materials and many instructional materials. The other teachers told me at the beginning of the year there was no stipend for supplies. The principal didn't mention if there were books available for use somewhere in the school or if someone could donate books, and I hadn't thought to ask. Did the other teachers have classroom libraries? I hadn't seen any.

True to his word, several days later I found a four-shelf bookcase parked inside my classroom. I pushed it to the rear of the room near the back door. This location made it accessible but out of the traffic pattern.

A few days later, three of my homeroom girls showed me some novels they owned that they had brought to school. I could tell from the start that they had been close friends for years, as they often chatted, wrote notes to each other, and chose each other for partners. Nadine, a pretty Caucasian girl with a lovely round face, dazzling smile, and beautiful sleek curly hair who I thought could be a model for Seventeen magazine, was holding several books from the Babysitter's Club series. Grace, an attractive long-faced, Caucasian girl with freckles, was holding Sweet Valley High books. Rachael, a cute fair-skinned girl-next-door type with a round face and straight blonde hair, was holding a couple Nancy Drew books. I thought all three of these girls dressed in their plaid uniform skirts with their cute legs and bobby socks could pass as cheerleaders for some youth basketball or football team.

"We'd like to put these on the shelf so that we can share them," they told me, pointing to the bookcase.

"That's great!" I replied. "I think that's a wonderful idea, and I really appreciate you sharing your own books with the entire class." We took turns placing the books on the bottom shelf. It accentuated the vacancy in the remainder of the bookcase.

Something must be right. These girls are showing initiative and good values. Did they come up with this idea themselves?

I prodded a little bit.

"So whose idea was it to have a classroom library?"

They looked at each other.

Looking down at the floor, Rachael confided, "My mom asked me what I was reading and why." She lifted her head and returned my gaze. "I showed her the book I have been bringing to class, and she asked why you don't have books available for us." I thought she sounded apologetic, but I could have been reading into it.

"Oh," I replied. "Well, as I said before, it was a good idea to have a classroom library." I looked at each girl. "I want you to feel comfortable enough to come to me first if you have any problems, questions or concerns. You let me know next time if you have any ideas or suggestions, okay?"

The girls nodded.

The homeroom bell rang, and there was no more time for conversation. I hadn't heard any more from the principal or the parents about the classroom library. It seemed to me as if it were the parents who had "jumped the gun" and gone directly to the principal. I didn't understand why they'd make such a big deal out of this and not take it up with me themselves. The principal had told me that a group of my students had come to him. So I presumed that the parents sent their children to the principal or asked the principal to take them aside to discuss the matter.

After only a few weeks, our book collection had grown literally from the ground up, from the bottom shelf to four full shelves as the students brought in more books and I stocked them with used books I bought. I found a local public library had used books for sale costing between twenty five cents to one dollar per book. I initially selected books with my previous knowledge of which were considered classic, popular, and enticing to middle schoolers. I had read many of these books myself over the years, my interest sparked by a young adult literature class I took in college as well as from my former students.

I bought books in all different genres hoping to appeal to as many students as possible. I stacked the shelves with books from Judy Blume (minus *Forever*, as that was not at all appropriate and would certainly never be acceptable in this school), Gary Paulsen, S.E. Hinton, Catherine Paterson, Paul Zindel, Richard Peck, Beverly Cleary, Robert Cormier,

Lois Duncan, Norma Fox Mazer, Cynthia Voight, Madeline L'Engle, Louis Sachar, and more. I never received a thank you from the principal or any of the parents. While the books were cheap, I did end up spending plenty of my own money.

I continued to frequent the used book sale, picking up books my students had expressed interest in. By the end of the school year, we had accumulated a couple hundred books!

We had outgrown our bookcase. I ended up purchasing self-assembly plastic shelving, and placing it underneath the chalkboard at the front of the room. Since there were only a couple of feet from the floor to the chalkboard ledge, I assembled the shelving so that we had multiple units of two shelves each. The shelves ended up stretching the length of the entire wall under the whole chalkboard to accommodate all these books. I had to initiate a check-out system to keep track of them all, especially when, on occasion, students would fail to return a book, as the library was open to my seventh and eighth grade students also.

I can proudly say that my students became very well-read. They shared these books with each other and discussed them on their own. They wrote very thoughtful entries in their journals, showing that they were thinking on a higher level than just about the facts in the book. They were able to critique the books and explain if the writing was good. They could compare books and compare books to movies. They created book projects (using time in class and at home) that were creative and informative. One of my favorites was a video made by Grace and Rachael where they acted out a couple scary scenes they wrote themselves to imitate the writing of R.L. Stine. It was fantastic!

We read many novels together, both orally and independently. My students became proficient, insightful and avid readers!

What I originally considered a travesty, turned out to be a boon for my students. While I didn't like the manner in which the message was delivered, having a classroom library helped create the literate students that any English teacher hopes for. I would have eventually added some type of library to my classroom without prompting, but perhaps it was better the way ours began since the students took ownership of the whole concept and helped it to materialize.

***

One day I was tired of packing lunch and desired a hot one. Mrs. A gave me directions to the school cafeteria, and I trudged through many a corridor to the complete other end of the building. I knew I found the right place when I heard the buzzing of hundreds of children's voices, the clinking of plates and silverware, and I could smell food. I had worked up an appetite just getting there!

As I set foot in the room, I was surprised, as it didn't look like the school cafeterias with which I was accustomed. This cafeteria had long tables and chairs instead of picnic table-type bench seating. There were colorful floor tiles instead of the institutional laminate. And, of course, there were religious pictures on the walls.

Instead of a long lunch line, in the center of the room was one small kitchen with a large open window. The lunch ladies were inside. It took me a minute to realize that one was a sixth grade parent. For all I knew, all the lunch ladies were parents. So I wondered if this was a volunteer position.

I said hello to my students as I walked past their tables. I grabbed a tray and stood in front of the glassless window. I expected to see a variety of steaming dishes, hot vegetables, and other prepared items on display awaiting hungry customers. There were none.

"Can I get a lunch?" I asked.

"Well what do you want?" one of the aproned ladies asked me curtly. She was a short, round woman, and I suspected that she was tired, cranky, and hot from standing near the oven.

"What do you have?"

In a recalcitrant manner, she recited a list as if I should already know, "Chicken nuggets, hot dogs, french fries, jello." I hadn't remembered seeing a lunch menu.

She glared at me.

"Those are the only choices?"

"That's it."

There was no backing down now. I had to pick something or go hungry.

"I'll have the chicken nuggets and french fries."

The cafeteria lady standing next to her reached into the oven, grabbed nuggets and fries, threw them on a paper plate, and shoved them across the window to me.

"Thanks," I said. As I took the tray, I noticed another parent, a thin, blonde woman standing inside the kitchen motionless. She had been glowering at me since the moment I came up to the counter. Her look combined with my growling stomach prompted me to whisk my tray away as fast as possible.

I hastened back to my room to eat my lunch alone. I had no desire to eat in the faculty room. After this experience, I went back to packing my lunch, as I was not inclined to eat children's food nor deal with the cafeteria ladies. If this was standard lunch fare, I understood why the teachers were hardly ever seen eating it. The blonde woman I knew I would encounter again outside of the cafeteria.

Chapter 5

On Earth as it is in Heaven

One morning after hall duty, I walked into my classroom which had the usual hum of voices like a low radio frequency. My homeroom students were in their seats, talking, completing last minute homework assignments, reading, and some even snoozing. Seated in the front row was the blonde cafeteria lady.

Her body was turned facing her daughter so that her legs were out in the aisle. She probably could have fit her legs underneath the desk, since she had a slender build. She wasn't bad looking, but I never really noticed her facial features since whenever I saw her I had to contend with her icy stare. Her arms were crossed. She was silent.

How did she get in here? I didn't see her come in. I was standing by the door. I can't believe she just plopped herself into a seat among the students. Why?

I stood there by the door. She didn't acknowledge me nor offer any explanation or excuse for her presence. I expected her to say something, anything, but she remained silent with her eyes locked on me. I expected her daughter or some of the students to explain her presence, but they continued chatting and didn't look in my direction.

I thought of saying, "May I help you?" I was deliberating when the morning announcements started. As always, everyone stood for the Lord's Prayer, including the cafeteria lady. I bowed my head. When I lifted my head and everyone was seated, she was glowering at me yet again. She didn't utter a word.

Oh, I'm not saying one word to her. She looks like she's ready for a fight, and I don't know what we're fighting about. They all must know why she is here. They certainly don't seem bothered by her. Even her daughter seems fine with it. Either it's not important enough to clue me in or nobody wants me to know what's going on. Very well then. "It's business as usual."

I walked over to my desk and took attendance. When I lifted my head again to ask a student for an absence note from yesterday, her seat was vacant. She was gone. It was only a matter of minutes before the students switched classes, and her daughter moved on to Mrs. A's room.

My sixth grade class came in, and I had to conduct my lesson. I needed to shake off the discomfort of an overt invasion by an undercover spy on a reconnaissance mission. I had no idea what she was fishing for.

Later that day I mentioned the incident to Mrs. A.

"One of the kids said that you told them not to say the Lord's Prayer."

"What??! That's ridiculous." At this point I didn't even care who said it or to whom.

"Yes, I know," she answered. "I wouldn't worry about it. Nobody took it seriously."

Nobody took it seriously? The cafeteria lady certainly did. And who knows how many other parents did once this rumor spreads. I hope she is satisfied. It should be obvious that I never said such a thing. I still can't get over that this lady took it upon herself to come right in and sit right down without asking or notifying me. Did she ask the principal for permission? I guess anybody is allowed in my room at any time. I suppose my door is always open, literally. Come right in everyone! No appointment or calling ahead necessary. We seat you immediately. Is there anything else we can do for you? Please see the secretary on your way out. Fill out a complaint form if you wish. Then I can get called into the principal's office again.

The next morning I felt like the pink panther sleuthing around. The theme song from the *Pink Panther* movies was in my head—ba dum, ba dum, ba dum, ba dum, ba dum, ba dummmmm, ba duuuummmmmm. (Instrumental composition by Henry Mancini, 1963.) I was more vigilant and observed each person as they entered my room. I looked each person up and down to make sure they weren't carrying any contraband or any devices such as "bugs" or hidden cameras with which their parents could monitor my class. I stood at the threshold and surveilled the room before entering, looking over every inch of the place to see if a parent was a stowaway in someone's backpack or tucked into my bookshelf. I peeked behind the wall to ensure no one was lurking in the coat area. I shut the door to my classroom in case someone tried to slip in after the children. I was determined that nobody was going to make it past me unnoticed.

Fortunately, my efforts were in vain. The cafeteria lady did not make another appearance. Nor did any other parents come to visit homeroom the rest of the year. Thankfully,

I never heard another word about this issue again, although I continued to scan the faces every morning and sometimes during my other classes. After several weeks with no unexpected visitors, my paranoia subsided, although it never completely vanished. Besides, I didn't really have time to play detective every day.

***

I was handling the vocabulary portion of Language Arts the way I had been taught in college. The students and I chose together unfamiliar words from the stories we read in class. I had a set format to follow for defining them and understanding how they are used. The students had already taken a quiz on our first set of words.

Mrs. A came in my room one day carrying a stack of small, orange, paperback books.

"These are vocabulary books for your eighth graders," she said, placing them on my desk. "Each student must complete the entire book. We use these every year. I usually give quizzes on Fridays."

As usual, she quickly departed.

Why didn't you tell me this at the beginning of the year? It's already October. Now I have to change my plans. I got the impression that her class had already been using them. I thought I had seen some of her eighth graders carrying them.

I picked up a workbook titled *Vocabulary Workshop (Expanded Edition, Level D)*. I opened it. Each unit contained twenty vocabulary words and their definitions, and within each unit were exercises to complete such as Synonyms,

Antonyms, and Completing the Sentence. At the end of each chapter was a review. Among the hundreds of words students were required to learn were staccato, untenable, perverse, impenitent, ad infinitum, sardonic, tenacious, and extemporaneous, to name a few of my least favorites. The word "ad nauseam" came into my head. Besides these words having nothing to do with anything I was teaching, the book was repetitious with the same boring exercises every chapter. My students were going to hate this! I could feel we would have the same argument every week over completing this.

There was no teacher's guide, or at least, I wasn't given one. I took an empty one and worked through the hundreds of exercises myself to make sure I had the correct answers. It took me a couple of weeks, as I worked on it when I wasn't grading papers, planning, ordering materials, creating bulletin boards, calling parents, sleeping, or eating.

I grew to hate this book more and more every week. One important rule I was taught was to not teach words in isolation. According to studies, the best way for students to learn new words is as they encounter them in literature or speech just as non-students do in everyday life. (This is called incidental word learning and learning words in context.) Providing random list of words is simply an exercise in memorization. Using this book went against what I believed was best practices for my students.

In addition, I felt these words were too difficult for my students. When I expressed all my concerns to Mrs. A., she told me that the principal said we are required to use these. I had no choice.

They are forcing me to teach here the same as they did in the 1950s. Neither the furniture nor the teaching practices have changed! We made the best of it. I give my students a lot of credit for not complaining about this after the first day. Most of them knew about this book either through older siblings or friends, so they weren't too surprised when I handed them out.

We completed some of the exercises in class either together or independently, and some I assigned as homework. Since I had to give a vocabulary grade, sometimes I would score an exercise. Occasionally, I used the review as a test, or I'd write my own. I created Jeopardy, Bingo, and other games using the words, and we'd take most of a class period playing the game as a review before the test.

It took us most of the school year to work through this book. We threw a party to celebrate when we were finished! The kids brought in food and drink. They could probably tell I was as happy as they were!

The students with good memorization skills learned the words. Some students struggled. I don't know how many of these words the kids retained after the tests. I can only hope that their vocabulary increased as a result. Perhaps some of the words stuck with them. On the other hand, even I can't remember the definitions of some of these words!

***

We were still in the first grading quarter when I assigned my eighth graders a specific story to read for homework. As I said before, I did not assign homework every night, and when I did, it was meaningful in some manner, such as reinforcing what we worked on in class, continuing an assignment, or perhaps preparation for the next day's work. This particular homework assignment was simply to read the short story, "Crime on Mars." There was no written work to complete. The story was 4 1/2 pages. So this assignment required each student to carry the heavy Prentice Hall textbook home.

I don't know what possessed me, but I made the drill the next day a pop quiz on the story. I suppose I wanted to check that they completed the homework. Or perhaps I wanted to make sure they remembered the story for the day's activity. Maybe I just needed a grade in my grade book. Or perhaps I felt as though the kids weren't taking my class seriously since they joked around a lot, and this quiz was a reminder that my class was important.

As a teacher, I wasn't often inclined to give pop quizzes. I had five simple questions about the story for them to answer. The rest of the class period I had planned for more work on the story.

When I revealed the quiz, I received a lot of dissent with students calling out all over the room.

"What? You're giving us a quiz on this?!"

"I can't take this quiz. I don't know the material."

"Why are you giving us a quiz? That's just mean!"

"I can't believe you're doing this to us!"

I couldn't believe what I was hearing, so I asked, "Please raise your hand if you read the story." I couldn't ask that they raise their hands if they had *not* read the story.

Thankfully they were being honest, but how much honesty could I ask for?

Not one out of twelve raised a hand. I was horrified.

I could hear the voices of the other teachers and the principal from the beginning of the year.

Pile on the homework. Load them up. The parents expect a lot of homework. All the teachers give homework every night.

I better stand my ground right now lest they riot and won't complete another homework assignment from me the rest of the year. So I mustered up the courage to deliver bad news.

"You are all receiving zeros for the homework, and we won't have the quiz."

I expected the complaints that followed.

I put up my hand. "Let me finish."

"You'll be able to make up the zero grade if you complete the homework tonight."

That quieted them a little.

Then I gave them time in class to read the story silently and complete the assignment I had originally intended to be group work. I was glad when a hush fell over the room as they all focused on the reading.

The homework assignment became the handout with questions that was meant to be completed in class. I explained to them how I was rearranging the assignments. I wanted them to understand how much more fun the class period would have been if they had followed directions and completed the homework.

I was nervous the next day. Since I had hall duty between every class, I watched them enter the room. I could see from the hallway that they all took their seats and worked on the daily drill. I had to rewrite the drill, the lesson for the day and all subsequent lessons. They had totally messed up my planning. I peeked in the room again.

So far, no riots. They're not standing on their desks yelling in protest, waving papers in the air, or tossing books off the shelves.

I walked in and told them they had one more minute to finish the drill.

I can't appear anxious, but I can't wait to find out if they did the homework. Deep breaths. Play it cool.

We reviewed the drill on sentences and sentence fragments, and then I asked them to pull out their homework. There was a lot of hustle and bustle, but after backpacks were rummaged and binders clicked open and shut, each student had a completed paper sitting on their desktops.

Thank heavens!! Wheww! I don't care if they didn't finish them, at least they each did something!

I almost turned around to thank the Virgin Mary on the wall!

Note to self: Don't assign a reading for homework ever again! But another pop quiz is still a possibility….

***

Several days later, one of the lower grade school teachers stopped me in the empty hallway after school. Her older daughter was in my eighth grade class, and her younger daughter was in my seventh grade class. I considered her a coworker, as I saw her in the faculty meetings. We never really talked to each other, much less discussed her girls. She appeared welcoming to me in the beginning.

"I heard what happened in your class," she said.

She must be talking about the eighth grade homework incident. What else could she mean? I guess, being a teacher herself, she is going to give me words of comfort. She'll probably tell me to hang in there; that the kids were testing me, but I'll be fine; or that I was right to give them all zeros for the assignment, but that she appreciated my giving them a second chance. That is what I would say.

I can't believe her eighth grader didn't complete the assignment either. I could see from day one that she is a top student. I can't tell her that though.

"Oh, you mean the homework assignment the other day for my eighth grade class?"

"That was a disaster."

"Huh? It wasn't that bad. I wouldn't worry about it," I said. "We're doing fine."

"I don't think you are."

"What? Why do you say that?"

"None of your students are doing what they are supposed to be doing."

"Oh, you mean completing that one homework assignment?"

"Apparently the students don't take you seriously or respect you as a teacher."

What? How untrue! How could she say that? What did she think was going on in my classroom? Things were going very well until this one homework disaster. I was so stunned I was speechless.

Before I could respond, she said, "Looks like you need some help."

She wants to help? Is she planning on coming into my classroom?
I don't think I need help, but I'm always open to try new things. Is she
sending me a mentor or something?

"It is obvious that you aren't prepared."

Did she just tell me that I'm not prepared for my classes after I go
home every night and work another three or four hours? Is she saying
that I'm not prepared to be a teacher? Is she actually blaming me for
the students not doing their work?

She was holding a stack of papers that she thrust toward
me.

"Here, I brought you some information. You need to
read these."

I took the papers.

As she walked away she said over her shoulder, "I hope
things improve in your classroom."

I stood there with my mouth open, holding the stack
of stapled, photocopied papers. I walked back to my classroom and sat at my desk.

What is she giving me? She must have found something about how
to motivate your students to complete assignments. Maybe this is about
being a first-year teacher which I'm really not. Perhaps she misunder-
stands that I am new to this school but not new to teaching.

I looked closer at the papers. They were articles from
several different educational and psychological journals.
They had titles like, "Revisiting Pedagogical Content
Knowledge: the Pedagogy of Content/the Content of
Pedagogy" and didn't pertain to me or my situation.

Where did she get these? Did she have these journal articles in her
house? Did she go to the library and photocopy them? They're probably

left over from her college days. Does she even know what she handed me?

Most people would have thrown the whole stack in the trash, but I put them in my bag to take home and read later. I thought maybe I could glean something from them.

As offended as I was, that night I sat down to read the articles. I read only the beginning of one before I gave up. I had the same experience with the second. In addition to droning on with vague educational lingo, the articles were totally irrelevant.

One of the articles incensed me even more. It was titled "Fearful Expectations and Avoidant Actions as Coeffects of Perceived Self-Inefficacy" by Albert Bandura of Stanford University published in *American Psychologist* in December of 1986. The abstract for the article reads:

Refutes I. Kirsch's (see record 1986-13702-001) suggestion that people take avoidant action because of expected fear. Contrary theoretical and empirical evidence is presented. (32 ref) (PsycINFO Database Record (c) 2012 APA, all rights reserved)

If I understood this article correctly and even just from the title, I felt she was saying to me that I was not a good teacher because of my own fears that I couldn't handle it. *How dare she.* And this was an article totally about psychology, not education. Was she analyzing me?

I attempted to read this long article. It begins:

The belief that fear controls avoidance behavior dies hard, despite growing evidence to the contrary. In a recent article, Kirsch (November, 1985) argued in favor of this view in his comments regarding the role of perceived self-efficacy in phobic dysfunctions. According to Kirsch, people take avoidant action because of expected fear.

The author is disputing the theory that fear causes avoidance behaviors. This was making even less sense. "Phobic dysfunctions"? She thinks I have a phobia and I'm dysfunctional?

I read several more paragraphs before becoming frustrated and tossing the article aside. I couldn't imagine what this woman was thinking. And by now, my eighth grade class was back on track. They seemed to enjoy my class and were working diligently, even though their work wasn't always complete or accurate. But I never expected perfection all the time. The important thing was that everyone seemed to be making an effort. I knew my students were learning and that I was doing a good job, even if nobody would ever say so. I didn't know why this woman couldn't see that in spite of one setback. How many other parents thought the same as she did?

I didn't discard the articles. I stored them away, but I never took them out again. The insulting parent-teacher never mentioned them after that. Thankfully, I had very little interaction with her for the remainder of the school year. Since she was in the lower school, I didn't see her often, and when I did, I sat as far from her as possible. I certainly didn't want to talk to her again! Who knows what she'd say to me next. A compliment was out of the question, I was sure.

***

Progress reports take as long to complete as report cards. A teacher has to calculate the averages for each student, and I had three subjects per student. So I spent hours at home working on them. I didn't agree with the school's grading system, as I thought it was harsh, but I abided by it.

In most schools, the grading scale is:

90–100% A
80–89% B
70–79% C
60–69% D
59 and below E

The grading scale at this school was:

97–100% A+
93–96% A
89–92% B+
85–88% B
80–84% C+
75–79% C
70–74% D
69 and below E

Obviously it's much harder to get a high grade, and it's easier to fail. I understood that the administration and staff wanted their students to be held to a higher standard, but I didn't think this was the way to go about it. I wondered if this was partially to blame for the next problem that came walking through my door.

It was still October when around 7:30 one morning I was writing the day's objective on my chalkboard. I was always in my classroom early to prepare for the day. I also enjoyed the quiet that would implode with the student stampede at 8:30 AM.

I was surprised when the mother of one of my seventh graders barged through my door. I had been given no notice or warning. She hadn't called me the day before to tell me she was coming. The school secretary, who wasn't even in the office yet, certainly did not announce her. Nobody escorted her down the hall or accompanied her to my room.

She was waving a pink paper in her hand. I recognized it as the progress report that had gone home the day before. She held it out to me.

"What's this?" she demanded.

"Good morning, Mrs. Jones. I think you know what that is. That's Christopher's progress report."

"Yes, but what are these grades?" she asked, shaking the paper beneath my nose as if she had Parkinsons or an untreated nervous condition. I could see she had written comments and circled certain words in red marker all over the paper. I was taught never to use red ink when evaluating a student's work because it is called "bleeding all over the paper." I felt like I was the student, and Mrs. Jones had bled all over my work.

"Well, I believe that you are aware that every English Language Arts student gets three grades," I explained. "One for literature, one for composition and one for vocabulary."

"I know that. But Christopher is getting C's."

"Yes, those are the grades he earned."

"Well that's not good enough."

"What do you mean?"

"He is an A/B student. He never gets grades below that."

"Well, have you talked to him? Christopher knows what he earned. His graded work has all been returned, and he is aware of his average to-date."

"Anything below a B is not satisfactory."

"Well that's just what a C means—satisfactory."

"My child is not just satisfactory. And why was I not warned about this?"

"What do you mean?"

"I didn't know his grades had fallen this low."

"Well, as I said, all graded work was returned, and Christopher knows what his average is."

"But I should have had some warning. You should have notified me."

"I am notifying you. That's what a progress report is for."

"You should have called me. You should have given me a call as soon as he got one grade below a B. Actually, I expect you to call me on a regular basis, at least once a week, and let me know what his average is."

This lady expects me to call her every week? Is she crazy?

"Well, as I said, this is your notification. We send out progress reports each quarter so that you will know how he is doing. I wasn't aware that you felt these grades are unsatisfactory. Maybe you would like to schedule a conference so we can go over them? Right now I'm getting ready for class."

"Christopher has to bring these grades up."

"He has time. This is only a progress report."

"Why do his grades look like this?"

"I wrote comments on the report." I pointed to the comments on the paper still in her hand.

"It says he missed a homework assignment. You should have notified me about that too."

Is this lady kidding me? I can't pick up the phone every time one of my 65 students misses an assignment or someone's grade falls below a B. Nor can I call parents once a week to give them updates. It's hard enough writing progress reports each quarter, and I can't write them any more often. She is so unrealistic. What does she think this is?

"Christopher just needs to apply himself more. He's perfectly capable. I'm sure if he makes more of an effort, he can raise his grade."

"Well his grades better be higher by the time report cards go out. This is unacceptable."

That's up to Christopher.

She continued, waving the paper at me again, "Next time you warn me before something like this is sent home."

"Progress reports will go out halfway through the next grading period as well."

"I expect a phone call if his grades are this low."

"I'll keep that in mind, but I can't promise anything. You are welcome to call the school and let me know if you need to speak with me," I said.

She gave me a blank look, turned on her heels, and walked out of the room.

Mrs. A came in later, missing Mrs. Jones by ten or more minutes. I told her what happened.

"Parents aren't supposed to be down here before school starts," she stated matter-of-factly. "I'll talk to Mr. Z about that." She didn't address the entire discussion about the progress report.

One morning the following week I was walking through the lobby on my way to the office as the students were entering the building. I noticed a sixth or seventh grader stationed by the corner like a sentinel. I figured this was a reaction to Mrs. Jones' intrusion. I would have preferred a U.S. Marine in full combat uniform with a rifle. I asked Mrs. A about the student, and she said that someone would be positioned there every morning to make sure students and parents went to the classrooms at the appropriate times. I thought that was a polite way of saying someone would always be standing guard.

Really? A kid? You are using kids as guards? An angry parent is going to mow them right over! You think one kid is going to stop a determined parent from walking through the lobby? And the kid is stationed there after students are already admitted into the building! What good is that? Any parent who is going to violate teachers' hours is going to show up before the kids. Maybe I should just be glad that somebody is taking action, even if I doubt it will work. I expect that I'll see more parents with complaints. And who knows at what hours other confrontations will take place. I hope I don't get assaulted. Thanks for keeping me so safe!

Chapter 6

Give us this day our daily bread

It was November, and the weather was turning colder. The whirlwind of leaves around the trees made a scenic, colorful view out my panoramic back windows that were worthy of a Van Gogh painting. I wish I could have enjoyed it more.

Added to my list of responsibilities and lessening my planning time several times a week was recess duty which meant supervising all the middle school children in the designated empty area of the front parking lot. We had to put on heavier jackets, so our coat room was crowded. We tried to stay warm outside. The kids would run around, playing tag or merely chasing after each other. Many students would stand and talk, bouncing or rubbing exposed hands to keep warm. I'd often have pleasant conversations with some of the girls during this time. One day two of my sixth graders huddled around me, and we talked about pierced ears and cosmetics. I'll never forget Monica saying in her sweet little voice, "Ms. B, you're so pretty. You don't need any make-up." I think I felt better about myself for several weeks after!

Soon recess would be held indoors, and I'd have kids from Mrs. A's class as well as my own crowded into my classroom. I'd offer them board games and puzzles to keep them occupied. Often the noise level would make me wish my closet was soundproof and I could lock myself in there. I would count the minutes until the end of recess.

It was around 10:30 one brisk morning when I was getting a dictionary off the back shelf to help one of my seventh grade students look up a word. A scraggly, bearded, partially toothless, wrinkled face appeared in the window. He wore a burgundy beanie above a smudged, dirty face. I nearly jumped out of my skin, dropping the dictionary. I had never seen anyone out my back window except for the lawn people. He started banging against the window and yelling. I wasn't sure if his words were slurred, or it was just the sound through the window, but I couldn't make out a word.

I stood there unresponsive. Panic had taken over my entire body so that what felt like ice in my veins kept me frozen to the spot. My mind was blank about what to do. It wouldn't even allow my feet to move. As I stated previously, I'm not good with emergencies. The students turned to see what the noise was.

Holy crap. He must be a vagrant. What does he want? Maybe he wants some food or shelter. I hope he doesn't break a window and come crawling into the room. Thank goodness my back door is always locked, although it's a flimsy hook and eye latch. (I eyed the door to ensure it was still locked.) I must protect the children at all costs.

He moved down the set of windows toward the door, banging each as he went. Then he started striking the back door. The door inched open slightly when he started yanking it. I stood by the door staring at the lock. Fortunately, it was holding. At this point I was trembling. I had it in my head to tell the children to run out of the room and save themselves. But nothing came out of my mouth.

"Who is that?" I heard Timothy say.

"What's going on?" I heard from Suzy.

My eyes were still on the door. I was petrified that the vagrant would burst into the room.

I was about to force my lips and tongue to work so that I could tell a child to go get help from the office when one of them yelled, "Ms. B, that's Paul Butler's dad!"

"What?"

"Yes, I've seen him before."

Are you sure?"

Brianna came over to me by the door.

"I'm sure, Ms. B. That's him. It's okay to open the door."

I was still too afraid. The man returned to the window and stood silently peering back at me, his eyes blinking like an animated computer graphic. At least he stopped banging and shouting.

Johnny agreed, "That *is* Paul's father."

"Open the door, Ms. B," Tina was telling me. "It's okay—really."

I trusted my students, so I timidly unlocked the door and opened it a crack. I was about to ask him what he wanted when the door came rushing toward me, almost knocking me off my feet.

"Thank you," he said breathlessly, stepping into the room. He was dressed in torn blue jeans and a denim coat. He looked like he could use a bath. He didn't seem to notice that I was plastered against the back shelving unit from where the door had pushed me.

By this point, most of the kids were out of their seats and standing around.

"Hi, Mr. Butler," one of the kids said.

"Hi, Jimmy," he responded.

Oh thank goodness they know each other, and this man actually is a parent. Wheww!

Relief took over my entire body so that my limbs and feet started working again, and I stood upright. My voice was also returning. Good thing I had a strong bladder, or I might have had an accident.

"I have Paul's lunch," he said turning toward me, holding up a wrinkled, tattered, brown lunch bag. "I don't want him to go hungry."

Really? All this over a lunch? Can't Paul buy lunch if he forgot his?

"Paul's not here," I said. "He went to his next class."

Thank goodness I can speak again, and my speech is making sense!

"Oh. Sorry to have bothered you. I'll just go to the office then," he said, walking through the classroom toward my front door.

Thank goodness he's leaving. I guess he knows how to get to the office. He certainly knew how to find my door. I guess he won't scare anyone else on the way. I'm glad he didn't ask me which class Paul is in now, as I wouldn't send him there. I wish he would have gone to the office through the front school door to begin with.

He stopped and looked back at me. "Sorry if I scared you."

Scared me? How about terrified me? I guess it was obvious. Maybe he actually noticed that my face turned as white as the Virgin Mary on the wall, and my curly hair uncurled!

"Next time, Mr. Butler, please use the front door of the school," I replied as composed and professional as possible.

I didn't see him the rest of the school year. When I told Mrs. A about the incident, she told me that the Butlers live on a nearby farm and don't have much money. So Paul couldn't buy his lunch if his father didn't bring it to school. She wasn't surprised about how Mr. Butler introduced himself. As usual, since all these teachers were familiar with these parents, someone could have given me a heads up about the Butler's situation.

***

By this point I had been boyfriendless for quite some time. I enjoyed dating more over the summer months when I wasn't working, even though I was usually taking a professional development class. I did want to eventually get married and have children of my own, even though I considered these students my own kids, of sorts.

I preferred to date Jewish men. I didn't feel like having a war with my father over dating someone who wasn't. Besides, I hadn't found anyone from another faith who was worth fighting for. Since I attended parties put on by Jewish singles groups, it made it easier to date Jewish men. I also felt my dad was right that it's just easier to stick with someone "of your own kind." I hadn't the inclination to date someone from another faith and try to explain my own religion to him. It was hard enough answering questions from my students.

During college when I was still living with my parents, I brought a non-Jewish boy home, and my father wouldn't let him in the house! At the time I thought that was a little too strict and close-minded. I thought I should be allowed to explore all my options and get to know people of all races and religions. But in my heart I could understand his thinking. One date could lead to a second which could lead to more and eventually marriage. So if it never starts, then there is no issue. Part of me appreciated his setting a limit and protecting me. I wasn't resentful as someone could be in that situation. And I never was rebellious. Possibly because of his behavior, after I moved out I stuck to dating men of my own faith. So his parenting technique worked!

One Saturday night I went to a Jewish singles event with a couple girlfriends. It was a game night hosted by the leader of a singles group with whom I was friendly. I knew several other people there as well. Two gentlemen were playing Monopoly, and one invited me to join the game. So I did. We talked about the game and then he told me he recognized me from our high school class. He said his friend who was playing with us was also a classmate. (His friend didn't say much of anything to me except "It's your turn.") I was surprised, since I didn't remember either of them. I went home later and looked them up in my yearbook. We had about 400 students in my high school class, and I didn't remember crossing paths with these two.

We exchanged telephone numbers that night, and he called me several days later. We began dating. We'd go out to dinner or to the movies on Friday and Saturday nights. I kept him company once while he was painting a room in his house. I did manage to spend time with him sometimes on weeknights, bringing papers to grade or other work.

One Friday night, I went with him to shop for carpet. It was late, and the carpet store was crowded. We had to wait a long time for a salesman.

"I have to sit down," I said, seating myself on a roll of carpet on the floor.

"Why?" Richard asked me.

"I'm tired," I replied.

"Why are you so tired?"

"It's been a long day."

"What did you do today that was so tiring?"

Are you kidding me? What did I do that was so tiring? You know what I do for a living. Do you think it's easy?

"I was teaching," I declared, defying him to continue down this detrimental path.

The carpet salesman finally came over and interrupted. Choosing carpet, getting a price and scheduling installation took another two hours. I couldn't wait to leave.

On the way home I closed my eyes in the passenger seat and leaned my head against the window.

"I really don't understand why you are so tired."

Oh no. Here we go again. He really wants to pursue this line of questioning.

"I've been on my feet all day," I answered, agitated.

"So? You should have been more awake to help me select the carpet. I'm really disappointed. I wanted your help."

"Really?...Look," I said. "You're an accountant. You get to sit at a desk all day. I spend all my time either standing or walking around the room. I hardly ever get to sit. And my dress shoes aren't that comfortable. You also didn't seem to have any problems knowing what carpet you wanted."

I closed my eyes, and we said nothing else the remainder of the car ride.

Does he get it, or is it that he just doesn't want to argue with me? I doubt he gets it. But I'm too tired to talk about it anymore. He's being stupid.

I remained angry about the whole conversation for the rest of our relationship. I knew any time I appeared without energy, we were going to have an argument. So I tried to be as well-rested as possible, although I didn't get to bed any earlier most nights. I tried to be more alert when I was with him. But having to do this made me resentful. I felt that it wasn't only him; so few people had any sympathy for what a teacher's life is like. In addition to not realizing we are on our feet all day, we work around the clock well beyond 3 PM and sometimes over the summer.

***

Mrs. A and many of the elementary school teachers had been putting their students' work on display in the hallway. Mrs. A hung up writing exercises her students did. I read some of them, and they were very good; however, I thought it was interesting that the writing was in response to something they read.

Mrs. A complained that any type of adhesive she used did not keep the papers attached to the wall. One morning I came to school and found wooden cork strips had been installed the entire length of both sides of the hallway.

She must have complained to the principal. I see that Mrs. A must usually get what she wants. Well, this isn't a bad addition to the school.

After Mrs. A hung her students' work from the cork, my side of the hallway looked empty. I decided it was time to hang some of my students' work.

They had written several good pieces so far. To teach writing and give each student a composition grade, I used a writing workshop format. In a writing workshop, students are permitted to complete any type of writing of their choice. Every student writes according to his or her own interests. The teacher offers examples, models writing, and guides the students through the writing process. Exposing students to a variety of literature assists in the process and integrates reading with writing. Students work together using peer review and teacher review to improve. Grammar, spelling, and punctuation are included at the latter end of the process during revision.

This type of teaching fosters a classroom learning environment of collaboration where students are independent, self-motivated, and involved. My students produced work that was well-above their perceived ability levels. Mrs. A appeared impressed, especially with a poem I exhibited from one of my sixth graders. Zachary had a learning disability in addition to physical limitations due to problems with his lungs and multiple hospitalizations. None of his former teachers expected much of him.

"Boy, I didn't know he had it in him," Mrs. A commented one day, pointing to his paper on the wall. We were standing in the vacant hallway after school.

"Yes, he wrote that entire piece himself."

"That's surprising. I hope the rest of his work this year is as good."

This was a real compliment, and probably the first I had received from her. I couldn't be happier, even though I felt as though she tried to put a damper on it by implying that he couldn't keep it up. He did though. All the students continued to produce work on this level throughout the school year. Not only were the students experiencing success and enjoying writing, but I knew I was being successful as a teacher. This knowledge kept me going throughout the year.

My students' work was so impressive that I created avenues for publication. I compiled their work in literary magazines by typing each student's work, photocopying them and binding them in spiral books. I distributed copies to the entire middle school. Students competed to create artwork for the covers, and I picked winners. I remember that seventh grader, Ethan, won the cover contest for one of the issues, as he was a talented cartoonist. For every issue,

I would hang each page of the magazine in the hallway. Later in the year, my students became reporters, editors and writers as they roamed the school interviewing, researching and writing. We published several school newspapers that year. We had a lot to be proud of.

Here is Zachary's poem that really impressed Mrs. A:

A is for Asthma

A is for asthma that's easy to see
even if you've never been in a spelling bee

S is for the slow bid machine I take
when I go to sleep and also when I wake

T is for triggers that start asthma up
and having an attack can be very rough

H is for help, a thing I need most
especially when I start to cough and choke

M is for medicine, a thing that I need
to keep me alive and to help me breathe

A is for air sacs down in my lungs
that help me breathe so I can run

Chapter 7

Close the door of hate
and open the door of love all over the world.
Let kindness come with every gift
and good desires with every greeting.

From "A Christmas Prayer" by Robert Louis Stevenson

Only a few more weeks, and it was winter break, or as everyone else called it, Christmas vacation. I couldn't wait to have two weeks off to sleep late, relax, go see a movie, spend time with family and friends, and, of course, as always, even on my vacation, do some lesson planning. I had such little time to work on lesson and unit plans that if I didn't do something, I'd have nothing to do with the kids when we returned in January. I could see it now when we returned on the first day. My sixth grade class would be seated in front of me, staring at me, looking at each other, wondering what was going on.

"Ms. B, where's the drill?"

"Oh, I didn't prepare one. I didn't prepare a lesson either. I decided I needed some rest, so I didn't do anything over winter break. I have no clue what we should do today. Does anyone have any suggestions?"

I could hear Tommy scream, "Let's have a party!!"

The rest of the class would respond, "Yes, let's have a party!"

Somebody would find a radio and turn on the music, and the kids would be dancing on their chairs. (Hopefully they wouldn't tip over, but if they did, they'd just think it was funny.) Somebody would go get her lunch and distribute chips and cookies to everyone.

I would just lean on my desk observing the chaos. After all, what could I do without a lesson plan?!

"Ms. B. Let's have a party every day!" Brian would exclaim.

"Yes, every day!" all the kids would shout.

That would be the end of my teaching career.

Teachers have no choice but to plan ahead. Often, certain materials such as films, audio-visual materials, and even sets of books need to be ordered ahead of time, either from the school library, public library, or a company. Although I had a pretty good collection of my own materials—posters, decorations, handouts, stories on tape, videotapes, reference materials, and other items (which I managed to cram into my small apartment), I did not have everything I needed. I also created a lot of my own materials which took a lot of time and planning. I still have a sofa stained with glitter glue from when I made a giant spinning wheel for a game. Sometimes I used the students' projects to decorate my classroom. The scenes my seventh graders created from *The Pearl* by John Steinbeck looked very attractive on the back ledge.

Some teachers decorated their rooms for Christmas, so it looked like all they were missing was a ham dinner and some eggnog. Tinsel, garlands, and bows adorned their bulletin boards, doors, walls, and windows. I wanted to join in the merriment and make my room look festive too without using actual Christmas decorations. I tried to find decorations that were winter-themed, so I ended up with snowflake window clings. That was the extent of my decorating—snowflakes stuck to my windows.

I wouldn't dare hang dreidel or menorah decorations, although I considered hanging decorations for Christmas, Chanukah and Kwanza altogether. I thought it would be good for students to recognize all these holidays, but I knew it wouldn't go over well. I didn't have it in me to fight for it. After all, I didn't want to make everyone afraid again that I was teaching about other religions, especially Judaism.

I walked into Mrs. A's room one day to ask her about ordering a book, and I noticed a different type of calendar in her room.

"What's that?" I asked, pointing to it.

"That's my advent calendar," she said.

"Advent? What's that?"

"You don't know what advent is? I keep forgetting you don't know anything. It's the countdown to Christmas."

Is that like the countdown to midnight on New Year's Eve? How many days ahead are you looking? I'm not going to ask. I sound ignorant enough.

"Oh," was all I said, and she didn't offer any further explanation. She must have thought she explained it well enough.

There was a small Christmas tree in the front lobby and a larger one in the vestibule by the new church. Since the new church space was so big, that tree was as tall as one you'd find in a forest. It was gleaming with decorations and a giant golden cross sitting atop. I thought it was attractive and festive. I saw it every time we went to church during the holiday season.

Boy, everything is going to look so bare when all these holiday decorations are removed. It didn't look bare before the holiday season. I didn't know you could stick Christmas decorations in every nook and cranny of this building!

After school one day, we were all crammed into the faculty room for a meeting to discuss winter programs. The music teacher mentioned that we needed to put her annual evening student musical performance on the calendar.

Oh no, I'm going to have to listen to two hours of Christmas songs, aren't I?

Everyone looked at the calendar, and they all decided on a date. I wrote it on my calendar as well. I heard it on the morning announcements, and I sent the flyers home with the kids. Nobody told me I had to be there, so I didn't attend. I guess this one wasn't mandatory, because I didn't get in trouble for not going.

During this meeting someone mentioned teachers having a Secret Santa.

Secret Santa? What are they going to have me do now? Do I have to dress up like Santa Claus? Or do they have Santa come in and I have to sit on his lap and tell him what I want for Christmas?! I don't like the sound of this.

"What's that?" I whispered to Mrs. A.

"You don't know what a Secret Santa is?" she asked incredulously.

I shook my head.

You pick a name out of a hat and leave little Christmas gifts for the person, but they don't know who it's from until the end.

I must have been in a tizzy because I didn't understand anything she said. *What's that? I give presents to whom? I have to put Christmas presents under someone's tree?*

"You do what?"

"You get a person's name and give them gifts in secret."

"But I don't know how to pick out Christmas gifts." My voice was getting higher along with my anxiety.

'They don't need to be Christmas gifts. They are just any type of small gift."

"Like what?"

"Oh, anything. Some people put pencils or lip gloss or things like that in someone's mailbox."

The foreign language teacher was walking a brown paper bag around, and everyone was picking a slip out of the bag.

She came to me.

The bag triggered my understanding. Everyone's names are in the bag. Is my name in there? How did my name get in there?

I just looked at her.

"It's your turn, Diane."

"No, thanks," I said. I didn't want to buy Christmas presents for someone, especially someone I most likely didn't know or didn't like. I wouldn't have any idea what to buy. And I wasn't sure I should participate in a Christmas tradition. I hadn't made the connection that it was only a gift exchange.

"You're not going to pick a name?" she asked.

"Diane, you should pick a name," I heard from behind me.

"It'll be fun," another voice behind me encouraged.

All eyes were on me, so I took a slip from the bag. After the teacher moved on to the next person, I opened up the paper so that no one else could see it. The name on the paper was Mrs. A! *Was this rigged?* I wasn't sure if I was happy about that because she was familiar or upset because I didn't want to buy her presents.

I looked over at her. She was busy talking with another teacher.

Does she know I drew her name? I don't care who drew mine. I don't want to buy Mrs. A presents, and I don't want someone forced into buying me presents. I don't want someone who most likely doesn't want me in the school to give me things. Besides, what would I get? Would I receive a bunch of gag gifts like a fake spider, or worse, nasty things? Maybe I'd get a bag of dog poop in my mailbox or itching powder.

A shiver went up my spine. I even felt an itch on my leg.

In spite of how I felt, for the next two weeks, I put holiday pencils, small candies, and other knick knacks in Mrs. A's mailbox. The gifts had to be small since the mailboxes were stackable shelving units only about an inch wide and a foot deep per slot. They were meant to hold only papers. Every so often I'd hear other teachers talking about the gifts they received and how much they liked them. I never heard Mrs. A mention receiving anything.

Did she get my gifts? Did someone else take them from her mailbox? Did she receive them and not like them? I thought I did a good job.

Like Ethel Rosenberg, a famous U.S. Jewish spy, I sneaked a peek at Mrs. A's mailbox at times to make sure she had received the gifts. I'd pretend to get something out of my empty mailbox and glance in hers. I looked at the other teachers'. Some still held little wrapped presents. The gifts were no longer in her mailbox, so I assumed she got them and nobody else was taking them. I didn't think these teachers stole from each other.

I received a few gifts from my Secret Santa. One day sitting on my desk was a small wrapped box containing a clear mug with a picture of a snowman wearing a sprig of holly in his black hat. I liked it even with the sprig of holly. I assumed it was too big to fit in my mailbox. Another day I found in my mailbox a tiny box of chocolates with a little gold bell on it. I loved it, as chocolate is one of my favorite foods!

One day Mrs. A came in my room while I was opening up a thin box I had found in my mailbox. Inside, wrapped in tissue paper, was an oven mitt with holly and berries on it.

As I took it out of the box, she commented, "Oh, that's a nice present."

She saw the disappointment on my face. "Don't you like it?"

"Well, it's a Christmas present," I said.

"What's wrong with that?"

"I celebrate Chanukah."

"So? It's an oven mitt that has a Christmas theme."

"Yes, but it's not something I would hang it in my kitchen," I said, putting the gift away.

She walked out of the room.

Why can't she understand that I don't celebrate Christmas and don't hang Christmas objects in my apartment? She wouldn't decorate her house with dreidels and menorahs. That was a strange reaction.

The religion teacher came by later and saw the oven mitt. She understood when I explained that I wouldn't use it. She was happy to take it, and I was glad she could use it. I didn't ask her if she knew who it was from. I didn't think she knew anyway.

When the gift exchange was over, Mrs. A told me she was my Secret Santa.

That explains it! Now I understand her reaction to the oven mitt.

"That's funny," I said, "because you were mine!"

I thought she would think it amusing that we had each other, but she didn't laugh or smile. She didn't thank me for any of the presents. I felt embarrassed by my reaction to her oven mitt, and I didn't want to sound ungrateful. Although, after some thought, I didn't feel terrible because there was no reason why she couldn't get me something that had a winter or Chanukah theme. She, of all people, knew I didn't want something that screamed Christmas! I also wondered if she was purposely trying to make me feel alienated or if she honestly felt that it was an appropriate gift.

***

I took my homeroom class to Mass the week before Christmas. I wasn't usually notified very far in advance which caused a disruption in my planning. I tried to keep all three of my classes on similar lessons every day to make it easier, but that was almost impossible with interruptions by the DARE officer, church services and other special programs throughout the year.

I was nervous about attending a Christmas service since I had never been to one, but then I could see it was like any other service we've attended. I found out later that there are masses on Christmas Eve and Christmas Day that are focused more on the holiday.

I always sat at the end of the pew or by myself depending on where the kids were situated. I didn't want to be a part of the service even though I had to be there, and I wanted to be able to make a quick exit if needed. I was zoning out when I heard something familiar. I tuned in to a reading from Jeremiah 31:31–34:

31 "The days are coming," declares the Lord,
"when I will make a new covenant
with the people of Israel
and with the people of Judah.
32 It will not be like the covenant
I made with their ancestors
when I took them by the hand
to lead them out of Egypt,
because they broke my covenant,
though I was a husband to[a]them,[b]"
declares the Lord.
33 "This is the covenant I will make with the people of Israel
after that time," declares the Lord.
"I will put my law in their minds
and write it on their hearts.

I will be their God,
and they will be my people.
34 No longer will they teach their neighbor,
or say to one another, 'Know the Lord,'
because they will all know me,
from the least of them to the greatest,"
declares the Lord.
"For I will forgive their wickedness
and will remember their sins no more."

Oh, right. I forgot they also read the Old Testament. This reading must be from there. So we believe some of the same things, I suppose. The school secretary was right. We did have something in common.

From my time in church, I had recognized other scriptures, particularly that of Adam and Eve as well as "The Lord is my Shepherd" prayer and a few lines from Psalm 103, "The Lord is compassionate and gracious, slow to anger, abounding in steadfast love..." I was always happy to hear something familiar.

But what are these lines from this reading actually saying?

In Hebrew School there wasn't a lot of Bible study. We learned the basic Bible stories, how to read Hebrew, the parts of the Torah (which is primarily the five books of Moses), and about the Sabbath and holidays and the accompanying prayers. I felt at a disadvantage being unfamiliar with the Bible.

I had learned about G-d's covenant with Abraham. (We put the dash in G-d so as not to write His name in vain.) Was there another covenant? I wasn't going to learn the Jewish perspective from where I was sitting. I did know that Jews considered only one covenant and anything else did not negate that. When the pastor started saying something about the new covenant pertaining to Jesus, it became obvious to me how our religious interpretations differ.

I guess we will have to agree to disagree on this. Now I can definitely see where our differences lie. I suppose some of these parents dislike me simply because I don't believe in Jesus. The note had said, "Jesus is the messiah, and don't you forget it."

At the end of the reading everyone uttered, "Thanks be to G-d" which I thought was a very nice response, but one I wasn't going to mimic. I liked how people shook hands and said "Peace be with you" at the end of each service. In the first service I attended, I hadn't expected this greeting. Nadine was the first to tentatively put her hand out to me with wide eyes as if to ask, "Is this okay?"

"Peace be with you," she said timidly.

I smiled, shook her hand, and responded in kind. Her face eased with relief, and she smiled back. As time went by, students and even a few teachers did this "exchange of peace" with me, and I thought it would be nice for each religion to practice this. (There is a Jewish greeting of "Shalom Aleichem" which means "Peace Unto You" with the response "Aleichem Shalom" meaning "Unto You Peace," but I don't recall ever hearing it.)

Whenever I left a church service, in spite of my reluctance to be there, my disagreement with the teachings, and a feeling of not belonging, part of me surprisingly felt peaceful. Perhaps it was the singing or the time for reflection. Or maybe it was just a nice break. I usually have a feeling of fulfillment after a synagogue service, but it wasn't the same feeling. Perhaps the difference had to do with timing; I'd go to synagogue on a Friday night or Saturday morning while the church service was in the middle of the day.

I thought it was good for the children to worship during school hours and learn their teachings. After all, we all had the same goal to be good people.

***

Three days before winter break, Mrs. A informed me that we don't do any real work the day before vacation.

"What?"

"There's no sense in trying to accomplish anything when they're all wired about the break."

That means another day lost. It's not break yet, so I don't know why we can't just work on what I planned. They concentrate just fine in my room.

"Well then what do we do?"

"We are keeping the kids in homeroom except for lunch, recess, and their specials, and we are throwing them a party."

They'll be with me in homeroom ALL day?! Thank goodness for lunch, recess, and specials. A party? We're throwing a party? I've never thrown a party for my class. I guess a holiday party isn't a bad idea. My kids should do something fun and not related to the curriculum for a change.

"That's a long time for a party," I commented.

"It goes by fast. We keep them occupied with popcorn and a Christmas movie and a holiday craft activity. One year we made Christmas cards and another year we made wreaths. But I don't want to do the same thing again. Your class can do the same craft as mine."

Thank goodness, because I have no idea what Christmas craft I could do. Thank goodness she is helping me out.

"You come up with the craft, and let me know what you decide. Make sure you buy enough supplies for both our classes."

She disappeared before I could protest.

Oh no!!! What kind of a bargain did I just strike? I think I got the short end of the stick! She always ends up sticking me with everything. She knows I know nothing about Christmas, and now I have to find a Christmas craft. Well I guess I can figure something out. I like doing crafts. I'll see what the craft store has.

I went to the local craft store on my way home. The pipe cleaners, popsicle sticks, pom-poms and paints didn't trigger any creative ideas for me. The poinsettias, Christmas gift wrap, and reindeer antlers didn't spark any Christmas spirit in me either. There were no kits with helpful ideas, and no sales person to ask for advice. I knew the lyrics to Christmas songs, had admired Christmas lights and decorations, and enjoyed a candy cane or two, but I never had a Christmas stocking, put cookies out for Santa, or had a Christmas tree. I had no idea what craft a child could do for the holiday.

I went to the public library next and took out a book on crafts. That also yielded nothing. While I was at the library, I rented a Christmas-related movie that I could watch with the kids. When it was time, we enjoyed *Home Alone*, the 20th Century Fox movie that stars Macauley Culkin who portrays a child mistakenly left behind when his family goes to

Paris for Christmas vacation. I felt it was a good compromise because it wasn't too Christmasy.

I told Mrs. A. The next day, "I couldn't come up with one idea for a holiday craft. I don't know what to do."

"I have an idea," she said. "I saw something in a magazine that we can use. Go back to the craft store and buy 50 Styrofoam balls, several assorted bags of sequins, a couple hundred straight pins, and some rolls of red ribbon. I'll explain later."

She couldn't just tell me that in the first place?

Thankfully the craft store had all those supplies in stock. I brought them in the next day.

"I'll make a sample," she said. "I suggest you do the same thing to show your students."

She took a Styrofoam ball and attached a loop of ribbon with the pins. Then she took one silver sequin and one pin. She put the pin through the sequin and then through the Styrofoam ball. She kept repeating this until part of the ball was covered.

"Looks good, doesn't it?" she asked, holding up the miniature disco ball.

"Looks good to me," I said.

Inside my head I could hear K.C. and the Sunshine Band singing, "I want to put on my, my, my, my, my boogie shoes...and boogie with you" in their 1975 song "Boogie Shoes." I knew this craft wasn't made for dancing.

She gave me half the supplies, and the next day my students were very focused on completing their homemade Christmas tree ornaments. Some students got very creative, using different colors and patterns. They worked quietly and seemed to enjoy it.

After I finished grading papers, I completed the royal blue sample ball that I had started. Perhaps I was thinking that blue was a Chanukah color. Although I couldn't figure out how to make it into a Chanukah decoration. I couldn't carve it into the shape of a dreidel. Nor could I use it to hold eight Chanukah candles.

I often did the same assignments I gave my students, sometimes to provide a model and other times so we could discuss our work. This time it was an activity to pass the time and spend downtime with my students. I was able to talk with them and ask them about the things they do outside of school. It was very pleasant.

Later that year when I read "The Pearl" with my seventh grade class, I created an entire underwater scene made of Sculpey clay that I put in an aquarium filled with water. I put it on display on my back ledge with all their projects. The principal came into my room to look over the projects and was surprised to find I made one.

Am I the only teacher who completes something to see how it would be for the students? Is that completely unheard of? I also like to show them I don't assign things randomly. Plus, I had fun!

"You did a project too? Mr. Z asked.

"Yes. I often complete assignments I give the kids. We talk to each other about what we did."

"Oh."

There was a moment of silence, so I waited for him to say something.

"Nice project you made."

Wow! I got a compliment!!! Although I just felt like I showed my parents my report card and was waiting for their approval. I'll take a compliment any way I can get it!

Not only did I go home that day with my own Christmas tree ornament and nowhere to hang it, I also had a ton of Christmas presents. I had to put them all on a cart and wheel them out the door since I couldn't carry them all.

I had no idea that in the days before Christmas just about every parent would send a gift. I was flattered that they thought of me, especially since every encounter I had with a parent gave me the impression I was thoroughly disliked. I was puzzled by the gifts, so I assumed that every parent was abiding by some holiday rule that mandated you give every teacher a gift. I could see that I wasn't the only teacher who received many presents.

I received cookies, candy, miniature teacher signs, coffee mugs, magnets, candles, soap, and a small, non-Christmas wreath. I was thrilled that the gifts were not religious in nature, and I could use or eat just about everything.

I particularly liked the wreath, a small heart made from little pieces of pink and red fabric pushed into a wire frame. I was curious about it, so I asked the boy who had handed it to me.

"This is beautiful," I said. "Where did it come from?"

"My mom," he answered.

"Did she buy it?"

"No, she made it."

"Really? She made this herself?"

"Yes. She made one for every teacher. Everyone got a different color.

"This must have taken her a long time."

"She likes to do it."

I was even more impressed that she had taken all those hours and used her own hands to make a special present for me. I didn't think the woman had ever spoken two words to me.

I wasn't sure I'd ever understand these parents.

My kitchen table filled with all the Christmas presents I received
(Photo taken by author)

Chapter 8

And Forgive Us Our Trespasses

It was a bitter cold morning in January, and freezing rain and sleet were tapping against our back windows a lot gentler than Paul Butler's father was rapping on them in the fall. The trees reminded me of zombies with their arms outstretched and their faces contorted and frozen in pain, the icicles hanging from their arms like folds of long sleeves. The public schools were closing early, and Mr. Z decided we were too. The announcement came around 9 A.M. with the wish that everyone gets home safely. The kids cheered and were thrilled, of course. Some of the teachers were calling their husbands to come pick them up; they were too scared to drive home themselves. Several teachers were gathered in the faculty room listening to the radio and using the phone. The announcer reported that the streets were littered with car accidents. I intended to drive myself home when a couple of teachers suggested I call my boyfriend and ask him to pick me up. I had told them he lived only a few miles from the school.

"Diane, you shouldn't drive yourself home. It's really dangerous out there," the science teacher warned me.

"I'm sure he'll come get you," the social studies teacher said.

"Call him," the science teacher insisted.

"Yes, call him," the social studies teacher encouraged.

After another teacher hung up the phone, I picked it up and dialed Richard at work.

"School is closing early," I told him. "Most of the teachers are getting picked up. I hear the roads are really bad. What are you doing? Are you leaving work?"

"They told us we can leave, so I'm going home."

"Oh....Can you pick me up?"

"Well, it's really out of my way."

Out of his way? Did he really just say that? I'm not far from his house. I'm an inconvenience? He doesn't want to help me? He doesn't care about my safety?

"But you're not far from my school."

"Yes, but then I have to pick you up and take you home. I'd be going out of my way."

"But I'm really scared to drive," I practically whined.

"I'm sure you'll be fine."

"I'd really feel better if you came to get me."

"Cynthia, your husband is here," I heard someone shout in the hallway.

"Please....," I begged Richard.

"You'll be fine. Call me when you get home."

"Okay," I said, hanging up the phone. Thankfully only the social studies teacher remained in the room, so I only had to suffer the embarrassment of abandonment in front

108

of her. I pretended as though everything was okay even though I felt like the freezing rain was inside my heart and my circulatory system, and when it melted, it would drip from my eye ducts.

"He's not coming to pick you up?"

"Nope. He doesn't think it's necessary."

"I hope he's right," she said. I hoped she wasn't going to tell everyone that my boyfriend is a real heel.

I drove home with my hands clenched to the steering wheel and my heart racing and pumping like the pistons in my engine. I drove under the speed limit, examining the roads for ice as I went along, as if I could see black ice before I slid on it. Traffic was slow anyway regardless of my driving. About an hour later, I pulled into my street and gingerly parallel parked. I was glad it was a nice big space, because I was afraid of sliding into another car.

I stepped out of my car and closed the door, carrying my purse and my school bag. After I took a few steps, my foot slid like I stepped on a banana peel, and I ended up on my buttocks. My bag fell, but my purse was still on my arm. I pushed myself up, grabbed my bag, and steadied myself on the patch of ice like a figure skater without skates. I looked around and was happy that nobody saw the fall. I'd already suffered enough embarrassment for one day. My behind was a little sore, but I was okay. I took another step forward and was able to glide across the street and down the sidewalk into my apartment building. Before I even took off my coat, hat and gloves, I called Richard to tell him I was home.

"See, I told you you'd be fine."

"Well not exactly. I fell on the ice after I got out of my car. It was really slippery. But I'm okay."

"Sorry to hear that. Well, you're home now."

"It wasn't easy. I really could have used a ride. I was scared to death the whole drive home. You hurt my feelings, and I was very embarrassed because everyone else got picked up. I was really disappointed you wouldn't come. "

"Sorry. It didn't sound like it was that big a deal. "

"I asked you repeatedly to come get me."

"I just didn't see any need to go out of my way."

"Well it doesn't seem like you really care about me. I could have been really hurt."

"Of course I care. But I still think you didn't need me to come get you."

"Yes, I did."

"You got home fine."

I didn't argue with him anymore, as it was getting me nowhere.

I'm not going to get through to him. He didn't see anything wrong with what he did. To me, this is grounds for a break-up. But I'll hang in there for now and hope that things get better. I doubt it though. How long is this relationship going to last?

***

My seventh grade student, Theresa, had missed over a month of school due to an ailment. She was the large student who had difficulty sitting in the tight chair the first day of school. She had been tutored at home, and the tutor passed along her grades which were all A's and B's. The grades Theresa received from me before she was absent had been significantly lower, some even D's. Her mother came in with the tutor to discuss her English grades.

The tutor came in first and sat in a student's chair, and Mrs. Johnson arrived several minutes later. She walked into the room and stood by the door.

"Please have a seat," I said.

She looked away from me and remained standing in the same spot.

She didn't respond to me. Doesn't she want to sit down? That's strange. Well, whatever makes her happy.

The tutor talked to me, and Mrs. Johnson listened. We discussed Theresa's grades. We agreed that a student usually performs better with one-on-one instruction.

When Mrs. Johnson had a question, she addressed the tutor. "How can her vocabulary grade be that different between the two of you? Aren't you teaching the same level words?"

"Yes," the tutor answered. "But I am working on them constantly with her. I drill her on the words every day."

"Yes," I said. "In class and at home she is responsible for studying the words herself. Perhaps you can help her study at home."

"I work," Mrs. Johnson uttered, looking down at the floor and never making eye contact with me.

"Perhaps we can find a study partner for her," I suggested, looking at Theresa's mother and then the tutor.

"That's a good idea," the tutor said. "Plus, I have been trying to teach her study skills. So that should help."

What is this woman's problem? Did I do something? She obviously has a problem with me.

The tutor thanked me, and Mrs. Johnson muttered something as she left. The tutor shook my hand and told me to call her if I needed anything else.

Did the tutor notice what just happened? How could you not? I wonder what she thought of that behavior.

I told Mrs. A what happened, and she said she didn't know Theresa's mother or why she acted that way. I told Mrs. E, the fifth grade teacher who had Theresa last year.

"Do you know why she'd act like that?" I asked.

"Oh, you know, I heard she did something like that a while back. We had a parent who was a Muslim, and she refused to sit next to her."

"Oh. Really?.....Thanks."

I don't know why I'm surprised. It always seems to boil down to the Jew factor. But still, the behavior was so inappropriate and mean. I can't believe she wouldn't even sit down. After all, I'm teaching HER child. As usual, I wish I had known ahead of time that there's a problem. I hope I never need to conference with her again.

***

I was on the yearbook committee. No teacher really wants to be on a committee, because it means extra work. During one of the first faculty meetings, I was informed that this was my assignment. This was a committee of two in charge of putting an entire yearbook together for the whole school. Who would I be assigned to do this project with? None other than Mrs. A, of course. Maybe we got the job simply because we were the English teachers.

I am not a procrastinator. To the contrary, I try to finish everything as early as possible. At the beginning of the school year, Mrs. A told me not to worry—that we would start working on the yearbook part way through the school year. Every so often, I'd touch base with her about it.

"What can I do?" I'd ask.

"Nothing yet. The kids haven't gotten their pictures taken yet."

After picture day I asked again.

"Nothing yet. The pictures aren't ready yet."

After the kids received their pictures, I asked again.

"There's nothing for you to do. Don't worry; I'll let you know."

"Well what needs to be done?" I inquired weeks later.

"The layout needs to be done. Don't worry about it right now."

It was February, and I still hadn't done a thing for this yearbook. I asked Mrs. A again what the plan was.

"We have to get the layout to the company by the first week in April."

"Well that's coming up soon! How do we do that?" I asked.

"I have everything at home," she said. "You'll have to come over my house."

"Okay. When should I do that?"

"We'll figure out a day."

Sometime after that Mrs. A and I were talking, and she mentioned she has a cat.

"Oh, I forgot. You're allergic to cats, aren't you?" she said.

"Yes."

"Well then I guess you can't come over my house to work on the yearbook."

"I guess not. I didn't realize you have a cat. Can we work on the yearbook at school instead?"

"No. I have everything at home. Don't worry about it. I'll get it done myself."

"But I don't want you to have to do the whole thing yourself," I pined.

"It'll be fine," she said.

"But I feel bad that I'm not helping."

"Don't worry about it. I'll get it done. I might get some students to help me."

Mrs. A produced a nice yearbook based on a "building connections" theme. She had a student create hand-drawn artwork for the cover and used bridge and construction related graphics throughout.

There is a page for each homeroom class with group photos. Underneath those, there is a portrait of each teacher. Mrs. A used her glamour shot, the photograph you have taken at a studio after they do your hair and makeup and give you a fake outfit to wear. She looks like a movie star.

My photograph was a picture a student took of me sitting at my desk. I had no nice clothes, no make-up, and my hair certainly wasn't done. I am slumped over my desk. It looks like the picture was taken on a day when I dragged myself in sick because it was too difficult to find a substitute and write substitute lesson plans. (At this school teachers called substitutes themselves. The office didn't do it for you. A teacher could go through a list of ten people before someone agreed to come in.)

My name is listed inside as being on the yearbook committee despite that I never laid one finger on that yearbook until I got my own copy. A couple teachers told Mrs. A and me what a nice job we did. I told them it was all Mrs. A, but they told me that I should accept the credit too. They didn't know that I truly had nothing to do with it. Mrs. A deliberately shut me out of this project. I assumed she didn't want to work with me nor did she want me over her house. I told myself that it was less work for me, and I should be happy about it.

Chapter 9

As we forgive those who trespass against us

It was a blustery winter day, and it felt like the hand of Old Man Winter kept pushing against my car the whole way to school. I pulled into the school parking lot later than usual. Cars were already parked, and parents were dropping off their kids in the carpool line. I pushed my car door wide open and held it with my foot to get out against the pressure of the wind. It was like fighting a sumo wrestler and trying to hold back his 200 pound loinclothed body. Fortunately I was winning this round.

I released my foot, and the wind shut my car door. I was clutching my lunch, my bag, and some large pieces of poster board that were flapping around like an injured bird. I fought for every step forward, and the wind pushed my hair upward, making it "stand on end." I saw my sixth-grade student, Rachael, getting out of her car. When I arrived at my classroom and put down my belongings, I tried to put myself back together.

A few days later I was walking around my classroom picking up trash while my seventh graders were working. I picked up a piece of loose leaf paper on the floor by Joseph's desk. This was the same desk where Rachael sits when her class is in my room. I glanced at the note and put it in my pocket.

Did I just see what I think I saw? Is this note about me? I don't have time for this. I can't read it now.

At lunch time, I took it out of my pocket and read it more closely.

I knew this was Rachael's. It was her handwriting, and I remembered that windy morning when I saw her in the parking lot. Since the note might be difficult to read, here is what it says:

This morning we were driving in and Mrs. B was getting out of her car and my mom says, "Oh, look, it's booger face. Oh my. I know how she did her hair this morning. She stuck her finger in a socket."

117

What should I be offended by first? That her mother is comparing me to mucus? And what a nice comment she made about my hair. Can I help the wind? Maybe next time I'll wear a hat!

I'm not going to say anything to anyone about the note, certainly not to Rachael. What purpose would that serve? She doesn't need to be reprimanded for writing it. It was a communication between her and a friend. I just wish she hadn't accidentally left it on my floor. I wonder if she'd be horrified if she knew I found it. Besides, I don't want to condemn the daughter for the sins of the mother. It wasn't Rachael's fault that her mother said those things. I didn't know Rachael's mother could be so nasty. Heck, I hardly know her at all. Now I certainly know how she feels about me. I hope that Rachael won't be influenced by her mother's poor judgment and attitude. Rachael is such a nice, well-behaved young lady. I hope she stays that way. I like working with her. I hope I never have to speak to her mother.

It turned out that eventually I had to talk to the woman. Rachael stayed after school one day because she wanted to work on her reading project. I told her she could do it at home, but she insisted. So we picked a day for her to stay.

On that day, nobody came to pick her up, so we went to the faculty room and called her house. Her mom answered the phone and was talking to Rachael about how she could get home.

Rachael turned to me and said, "My mother wants to know if you can drop me off at home since I live not far from here."

This doesn't sound like a good idea. In a public school, this would never fly. But things work differently around here. It's a small, tightly-knit community, and if I say no, everyone is going to think I'm terrible.

I took the phone and talked to her mother who persuaded me to take her home. In those days you didn't need a signed permission form to drive a student. Although if this happened today, I definitely would not agree to it. It is too chancy if something should happen, and there is always the liability issue.

When we arrived at her house, her mother invited me in!

Come in? Is she just being hospitable? I'd rather not.

She asked again and practically took my arm and pulled me in. She asked me to take a seat.

Come in and sit down? I know this woman doesn't even like me. What does she want? Why is she being so friendly? There's no way I'm sitting down with this lady.

"I really have to go."

"How is Rachael's project going?" she asked.

"It's going very well. Rachael has some good ideas and is working very hard on it."

"Do you think she'll get a good grade?"

"Of course. Anybody who puts that much into it is going to do well, I'm sure."

Is that what this is all about? She wants to find out about her grades?

All I could think about from the moment I walked in the door was the note. I almost felt like I could read her mind and that inside her head she was calling me booger face and thinking about how she didn't like what I was wearing or how my hair looked today.

"Would you like a drink of water?" she asked.

I feel like a mouse facing a trap, and she is putting out cheese as bait. I'm not taking it. What is she hoping to catch me doing? Is she waiting for me to say something wrong? What is her end game here? I'm not staying long enough to find out.

"I really have to leave," I said, and I walked toward the door.

As I opened the door, I said, "Thank you very much for your hospitality."

***

"This isn't working out," Richard said to me when he was driving me home one day. "Maybe we should break up."

"Break up?"

I knew things weren't going well, but I didn't think it was that bad, even after the arguments about the carpet store and picking me up from school on that icy day. I didn't want to break up.

"Yes. I think we are two totally different people, and I don't feel like our relationship is going the way it should."

"The way it should?"

"Well, for one thing, you want children, and I don't."

"I'm not totally sure about that yet," I said. I thought if I cared for him enough, maybe I'd change my mind—or vice versa.

"Well, it just seems like we are at odds a lot."

"Every relationship has its problems," I said. "That doesn't mean you stop trying."

Maybe I shouldn't have tried to pressure him into introducing me to his parents. It didn't matter anyway, since I knew he had no intention of letting me meet them.

"You're right," he said. "Why don't we give it another shot?"

"Okay," I said, feeling very deflated.

Why did I say all that? I shouldn't have changed his mind if he wants to break up. I don't want to be with someone who doesn't want to be with me. But I really don't want to break up with him.

From that point on, I felt like I was on probation. I knew better. I had previous relationships where a second try never worked. It might work in a marriage, but it rarely works in a non-committed relationship. I should have agreed to the break-up. I was only delaying the inevitable and causing myself more heartbreak.

***

I find that some of the best units are ones where the students teach the class. I was able to include this in our unit "Fact or Fiction." Most students love to do it, and they really pay attention to each other. They love to write on the chalkboard and the overhead. They enjoy being the knowledgeable leader. We had been reading essays, and I had them form groups and create presentations on the topic of the essays they read. Their presentations were informative, and they delved into the subject matter, asking terrific questions and having in-depth discussions. One seventh grade group tackled an essay written about the artist, Winslow Homer, and I think an art appreciation class couldn't have had a better discussion. They were so detailed about the artist, they were discussing his brush strokes!

At the end of this literature unit, I gave an essay test. One might think that students in middle school aren't ready, but with proper teaching and practice, students can write excellent essays. Some of them sounded like they were ready for college! For this test students read a non-fiction selection and wrote a complete essay on how it is a work of non-fiction. The students were able to critique the work, and they wrote topic sentences and supporting details in paragraph form. I was so proud of them when I graded their tests. It was more work for me to grade this type of test, but it was well worth it. My students were becoming independent critical thinkers and good writers at the same time!

Here are the questions I asked for the "Fact or Fiction" test in order for them to write one complete essay:

1. What is non-fiction, and how is this selection a work of non-fiction?

2. How were you affected by the selection?

3. Which classification/category of non-fiction does the selection fall into? Explain.

4. What is the author's general purpose for writing? specific purpose for writing? Explain.

5. What techniques does the author use to accomplish his or her purpose and how does he or she use them?

6. How does the author support his or her main idea of the selection? Remember to mention what the main idea is. Does the main idea fit the purpose of the essay? How does the author arrange the support of the essay?

7. Is the essay appropriate to a content area? Explain which content area and how the essay is appropriate for it.

8. Examine, explain, and evaluate the selection. Be sure to support your answer. Include what was good about the essay as well as what you did not like about it.

Isn't it impressive that they could answer all this independently on a work they had never read before? Their essay tests were fabulous!

Our journal writing also helped promote this type of writing and thinking. Here is a critique one of my seventh grade students wrote for a book she read that shows good critical thinking skills:

> The book I read is a called, Weasel, by Cynthia DeFELICE. I liked some parts, such as the historic placing, the Indians and heritage, and the memorable signs and symbols. One example of a historic placing was running the Indians off their own land. An example of a memorable sign was the letters and gifts that Erza, a white man whose Indian wife was killed by a raciest setter, left to Nathan and his family. Another example I liked was signs and symbols, such as the mother's locket. Unfortunately she died and left the father with two children, Molly and Nathan. The most heart warming part was the way the family cared about each other.
> I disliked the character Weasel, a man who killed living things including people for the game of it, because of his negative attitude toward living things. The reasons for disliking Weasel was because of his meanness, scariness, and rudeness. He actually cut off peoples' tongues,and left people to die in traps.
> This whole book was written very well and stated lots of history. I loved it, but I didn't read this book at night, for I dreamed too much.

Can you see how well thought out that is?

***

I was required to come to school in the evening for certain occasions. This particular night the middle school teachers were required to attend a Parent-Teacher

Association (PTA) meeting for the middle school. I was exhausted from a full day of teaching, but I went out to find dinner and returned for the meeting. We sat in the music room, and it was so jam packed that we were squeezed in as close together as the keys on a piano. It also felt warm from all the body heat. It looked like every middle school parent showed up.

The social studies teacher was leading the meeting. They were discussing something about the school board. I didn't even know there was a school board. I didn't know what a school board is. The business didn't pertain to me and I was tired, so I wasn't really listening. It was about ten minutes into the meeting when a parent raised his hand, and the social studies teacher acknowledged him. I couldn't see who it was behind all the heads, and I was on the other side of the room.

"I'd like to know why Ms. B gave my son detention. He didn't deserve it."

"What?" several people uttered, including the social studies teacher.

"The detention—she gave him a detention."

"That isn't relevant to what we are discussing."

Right on! You tell him, sister!

"I don't care. I'd like to know why he got it."

The social studies teacher asked, "Doesn't the detention slip tell you?" She never looked in my direction.

"Yes, but I don't think it's true. He didn't deserve it."

"Well, you'll need to discuss that another time with Ms. B."

Right again! Don't let him get away with this.

124

"No, I want to discuss it now. I think everyone should hear it. Why did my son get a detention he didn't deserve?"

People near me turned to look at me. I couldn't believe what I was hearing. This man was actually attacking me in front of all the parents and my colleagues. I just sat there motionless, adrift on a lonely sea with the wind taken out of my sails. Nobody was coming to my rescue.

I could get up and walk out, but then I look like a coward. I could stand up and speak out, but I'm not going to argue. I'm not going to give in to this. The best thing I can do is say nothing. I have to hope somebody puts an end to this.

Nobody answered him. I wondered why nobody stepped in to tell this parent how inappropriate he was. I was surprised he didn't stand up and point to me. Maybe he wasn't sure exactly where I was sitting.

He continued, "The detention said my son was disrupting class by constantly talking. Why would somebody get a detention for that? There are other ways to deal with that."

The social studies teacher shrugged.

She can't stick up for me? Why isn't she answering him? Why isn't she telling him that students get detention for disrupting class? This detention is obviously justified.

No one answered.

He continued, "My son is always well-behaved, and I don't appreciate him being accused of things he didn't do. I think someone should look into the way Ms. B teaches."

Everyone was silent.

How long are they going to let this guy go on? This is ridiculous. Are they waiting for me to say something, because I'm not going to address this in the middle of a PTA meeting. What audacity this man has. I refuse to respond.

I sat there with my lips tightly closed. Several parents were looking at me. My face felt red hot with embarrassment and anger.

The man continued, never standing up to look me in the face. "Ms. B is unfair. Who else's child got a detention from her who didn't deserve it?"

Nobody answered. Thank goodness, because I was waiting for a riot. I could only imagine what would happen if others joined in. Somebody might have to call the police to break up the melee. My life might be at stake.

Even more parents were looking at me now. I was still frozen in disbelief. I was determined to not acknowledge this accusation. I probably looked like I wanted to cry, because people tell me that's how I look when I'm angry.

Finally the social studies teacher said, "I think we need to get back on topic. Does anyone else have any questions for the school board?"

No one replied.

"Well then our meeting is adjourned. Thank you everyone for coming."

I suspected there may have been more business to conduct, but she felt she needed to shut this guy down. Thank goodness I was sitting in the back so I could be the first person to leave. I don't think anyone was going to dare stand between me and the door. I departed as quickly as possible, not looking back over my shoulder until my hand was on the door to exit the school. Then I made sure that man wasn't behind me when I got to my car. I slammed the gas pedal and "peeled wheels" as fast as I could out of the parking lot. I even checked my rear view mirror several times on the way home to make sure I wasn't followed. I was a little shaky on the drive home, but then the anger washed over me, and I firmly gripped the steering wheel and gritted my teeth. Oh, what nerve that man had! And what is wrong with all those people?

I expected Mrs. A or another teacher at school to approach me and tell me how sorry she was that the whole incident happened. Nobody mentioned it. Nobody tried to comfort me. I decided to not bring it up. Obviously nobody wanted to take sides or support me in any way.

That nasty parent never contacted me to discuss the detention. Perhaps he had no interest in talking to me face-to-face, or maybe he was a coward. The student never served the detention, and I didn't pursue it. I could only imagine what the parent would do if I followed up. I was sure the principal wouldn't take any action on my behalf.

I would never understand why everyone let this man continue to attack me. I felt like everyone had a grudge to bear with me, even if it was just because I was teaching there.

Chapter 10

And lead us not into temptation

It was around 8:30 A.M. on a Saturday when my home phone rang.

"Who's calling me this early?" I wondered, as I picked up the phone on my nightstand. I had been awake, but I didn't want to get out of bed. I was enjoying a leisurely morning.

"Hello?"

I heard deep breaths.

"Hello?"

There were more deep breaths on the other end.

Oh my goodness, I recognize that sound. I don't think this is a prank call. I can't believe I recognize somebody's breathing. I can actually identify this person. It's one of my students! I've been spending too much time with these kids!!!

"Monica, is that you?"

"Ms. B, how did you know it was me?!"

"I recognized the sound. Why are you calling me on a weekend, and why didn't you answer?"

"I was thinking that I shouldn't bother you."

"Well it's a little late for that. How did you get my number?"

"I looked it up in the phone book."

"My number is unlisted."

"Well I found it in the local telephone directory."

The local directory? The small directory for a cluster of nearby cities? I'm going to have to check that out and see if I can get my phone number removed. I didn't realize a student could call me at home.

"Okay. What can I do for you?"

"Well, I was thinking....I came up with a great idea for your bulletin board."

"You're calling because of my bulletin board?"

"Yeah, well...I know you wanted ideas for it."

"That's terrific, Monica, but can't this wait until Monday?"

"Yes, but I really want to tell you what I came up with. I came up with a whole underwater scene we can do with fish and —

"That sounds great. But can you explain it all to me in school?"

"Okay. I'd like to work on it. I'd like to do the whole thing. Courtney said she wants to help too. I can stay after school every day next week to work on it."

"I appreciate the help, and I admire your dedication, but we can figure it all out in school. I'd have to get permission from your parents. Maybe we can find time during school to work on it. We'll talk about it on Monday. Okay?"

"Okay. Thanks for listening, Ms. B."

"You're welcome. See you Monday."

"Okay. Bye."

Monica is such a sweet girl. But sometimes she's a little overeager! Or was it perhaps that she just wanted a friendly person to talk to? If so, I botched that up. I shouldn't have rushed her off the phone. I hope she didn't need anything more. I hope I wasn't rude. I'm with them for so many hours every day. I just want a little time to myself this weekend. I hope that wasn't too horrible. I'll talk to her on Monday to make sure everything is okay.

Everything was okay with Monica. She and Courtney helped me put up a new bulletin board during several lunch periods. It didn't have any fish. It did have grass and flowers. They had fun cutting up green paper for grass. They enjoyed hanging around and chatting, as those two were always quite the talkers. They were the ones who usually talked to me during recess. If I ever needed company, those two were available. I hoped they would never change. I just hoped that Monica would learn how to stay within certain boundaries with her relationships. She could get into a lot of trouble if she kept on this path of inappropriate calling!

***

It was first period on a Monday in March, and I planned on teaching my sixth graders mythology. About five minutes into the class period as we were finishing the drill, which consisted of two questions to get them thinking about these types of stories, Mr. Z walked in and sat down. Teachers get observed once or twice a year, but usually it is a formal observation where there is advanced notice. Teachers plan to give the observer a copy of the lesson plan as well as doing something special during the lesson. Sometimes, though, an administrator pops in for an informal observation which is usually only for a few minutes or part of a class period. Observations are unlike performance evaluations at most other jobs. With teaching, the administrator watches a lesson and writes notes. It's nerve-wracking. It's like being on stage. The teacher has no control over whether the students cooperate. Sometimes they act up just to be mean. But I was always very fortunate. My students were usually "good as gold." If I had a scheduled observation, I'd let them know ahead of time. They deserved a warning. And no matter what I said, they always knew that I was the one being evaluated.

I didn't have any scheduled observations this school year which I found to be unusual. But I wasn't going to complain! The principal had come in my room months before during my planning period and asked to see my lesson plans as if it had occurred to him at the last minute that he is supposed to be checking on me. I gave him my book of lesson plans plus my reading journal (as I kept one just as the students do). I had very detailed lesson plans which were probably more detailed than most teachers'. I was a student of an excellent college professor who believed that teachers should write scripts so they know exactly what they are going to say during a lesson. As time went on, I didn't write full scripts, but I did write a lot of details that I kept along with all my handouts, transparencies and other instructional materials. In addition, I didn't handwrite my lessons; I typed them on my computer and printed them out. I kept all my lessons in binders organized by grade and unit in case I wanted to reuse part of a lesson.

Mr. Z returned my lesson plan binder to me with only one comment. "I really liked the notes you wrote after each lesson. They were very detailed. I especially liked the one you wrote about how the lesson didn't go as well as you had hoped, but you knew how to fix it for next time."

"Oh. Okay. Thanks," I said, taking the binder from him.

That's it? All the blood, sweat and tears I put into these lessons, and he only liked my hand written notes? He has nothing else to say?

When Mr. Z walked in my room that day, sat down, and pulled out his notepad and pen, it was obviously an observation, and it unnerved me. I felt he could have given me some notification, even for an informal observation, especially because he stayed the entire 90 minute class period. Thank goodness I had an interesting lesson planned. He could have walked in on a day when there wasn't much to see if the children were writing or having a test or some other quiet activity.

For this lesson, we were reading an introduction to mythology and then reading together the myth of Arachne. (This is the story of the woman who spun thread so well that the goddess Athene was jealous and turned her into a spider.) I had the kids do some journal writing and other thought-provoking activities. I had a picture of women working at a loom, and I walked the picture around the room so everyone could get a close look at it before doing a think-pair-share, discussing with each other what they thought was pictured. Mr. Z took a good look at the picture, and wrote some notes. However, I doubt the notes were about the picture, but more about my teaching.

When class was over, he said goodbye and left. He didn't say anything else. I never got any type of write-up about my observation. He never called me into his office to discuss it. I never received any feedback of any kind. As a matter of fact, I never received any written feedback the entire school year.

Did someone complain, and he came in to check on me? Or was this a regular observation? Was no news good news? Did this mean that he was happy with everything he saw? Could he not tell me that? I could use some encouragement. Isn't it required for a teacher to get a written evaluation at least once a year? What did I have to show future employers? I could ask him for an evaluation, but what if I'm asking for trouble. He might write something I'm unhappy with. I'll just let it go.

***

During an after-school meeting with the middle school teachers, the group decided that any kids who got detention would serve it with a teacher on duty and not necessarily the teacher who assigned it. They decided that we would rotate detention duty between us on a set day of the week. I wasn't fond of the idea, but they all agreed, so I went along with it. I had been just fine staying after school and having my own students serve detention with me. I knew the kids, and it gave us an opportunity to talk.

Did this have anything to do with the kids who refused to serve detention with me? If so, I don't think this is going to solve the problem.

133

Mrs. A had given me a paper for the detained kids to copy. It was a couple of paragraphs with an apology and statements about behavior improvements. It was a blanket essay that covered everyone, no matter what the indiscretion. Each teacher decided how many times the student would copy it. Again, I felt like this was an assignment they've used since the 1950s, but, again, I went along with it. In the past when I gave a detention, I had students sit in my room for a good long time before I would speak with them. It's actually much more difficult for a kid to sit with nothing to do. They hate it. I told them to just sit and think. They would sit and stare at the ceiling. Some would put their heads on the desks. Some looked like they were thinking so hard they would come up with the cure for cancer. No matter what they did, they all looked totally miserable. I secretly called it Ms. B's solitary confinement. They couldn't wait to break out of prison, when we were finished talking. Rarely did they earn another detention with me. This essay writing was much less effective. And why have them write a bunch of words they probably don't believe? It's telling them what to say. What do they learn from that?

When it came time for my detention duty, the science teacher told me that Nicholas had done something unsafe in her science lab, and that his detention was scheduled for Saturday.

What? Saturday? He is serving his detention on a Saturday? You expect me to come in on a Saturday? You have to be kidding me!!! It's a good thing I'm not Orthodox, because Orthodox Jews do no work or travel in a car on Saturdays.

"I know it's a little unusual to give a detention on Saturday," she said, "but that was the only day I could get him."

If you weren't a former nun and I didn't like you, I may not even believe you.

"I know it's a lot to ask, Diane, but I'd really appreciate it if you could give him this detention. I'd do it myself, but I have a commitment on Saturday that I can't get out of."

How do I get myself into these situations?

"Well, I don't know. I have a lot to do on Saturday."

"Please, Diane. Nicholas really needs to be taught a lesson after what he did. I'd really appreciate it. I'll take two of your detention duties if you can do this."

Serving a Saturday detention is going to teach Nicholas a lesson? Well, I didn't really have any plans on Saturday. And I wouldn't mind skipping some detention duties.

"Okay, I'll do it."

"Thank you so much. I really appreciate it. On Friday I'll give you the keys to the school and the instructions for the alarm. You'll have to turn it off."

Alarm? We have an alarm? I don't know how to work an alarm! I've never handled an alarm in my life. Oh dear. I don't like the sound of this.

When Friday came, she gave me the keys to the front door and a yellow sticky note with the instructions and the alarm code.

"Just follow the directions for the alarm, and you'll be fine. There won't be anybody else around if the alarm should happen to go off, so you have to be really careful."

There won't be anyone around? There's nobody if I need help? It's just Nicholas and me? Should I really be in this building alone with a student? I guess if I mess up, the police and the fire department will be at the front door. Oh boy.

"Oh, and I have something for Nicholas to do."

He's not writing the usual scripted composition everyone uses?

"You know that we are preparing for our production of *The Wizard of Oz*. You were there for some of the after-school auditions. "

Yes, and thank goodness they only asked me for my opinion and not to do anything else.

I nodded my head.

"Well, we have a curtain we need to use, and we are putting the grommets on it along the top. I need Nicholas to hammer the grommets."

What? Hammer grommets? I don't even know how to do that. This is some detention.

"He already knows how to do it; I showed him. It takes a long time to do one grommet, so I only expect him to get a handful done tomorrow. The curtain is behind the stage along with the tools. Thank you again, Diane. I really appreciate it."

Saturday morning came, and Nicholas was waiting for me outside the front door. Apparently he had already been dropped off and nobody waited to make sure he got inside. He was a tall, thin, Caucasian eighth grader with curly light brown hair. Mrs. A had him for English Language Arts. I barely had any interaction with the boy until now.

I had only a minute or two to open the door, run across the lobby, get to the alarm panel, punch in the code and hit the right buttons to shut off the alarm. Nicholas was by my side the entire time. I explained to him what had to be done. I unlocked the door, and we ran across the lobby to the alarm panel as it was beeping. I asked him not to watch because I didn't want him to learn the code. I had the paper in my hand, and I punched the numbers and the keys that were listed. The alarm kept beeping. It wouldn't disarm!!!

Oh crap. Think fast!! Stay calm. I better do it again.

My heart was pounding and the yellow sticky note was shaking in my hand, but I pushed the buttons again. The alarm wouldn't turn off! Nicholas turned around and saw what was happening. I'm sure the panicked look on my face along with the incessant beeping noise was a sure clue we were going to be arrested and charged with robbery when the police pulled up. He asked me if he could try, and I said yes, since I was desperate. At that point, I didn't care if I got in trouble for giving him the alarm code. He followed the directions, and again, the low warning beep was still sounding.

Then the low beep turned into a high-pitched screeching siren that broadcast into every nook and crevice of the empty hallways and classrooms. We stood there in the lobby with our hands over our ears waiting for the cops to come.

Now we've done it. We're probably going to be arrested and taken to jail, because I have no identification that says that I'm a teacher in this school. Maybe they won't believe me, as I'll probably sound ridiculous telling them that I'm here to give this kid a Saturday detention. Who really does that? The only time I've ever heard of it is in the movie, The Breakfast Club, *and that detention didn't go well either. Plus, there's nobody here to back up my story. And I don't have*

137

anybody's phone number to call. Why did I agree to this? How long is this noise going to continue? I wonder if the police can turn it off.

There were no police cars, no ambulances, no emergency vehicles of any kind pulling up by the front door.

Is anybody coming? Doesn't anybody care that this alarm is going off? Is the alarm just to scare burglars away, but nobody really comes to take care of it? Will it just continue until tomorrow? Doesn't the noise bother the neighbors? Wouldn't somebody call it in?

About two minutes later a man in a security uniform walked through the front door. He must have parked out of view from the front door. He had let himself in with his own key, I supposed. He looked at us, walked over to the control panel, punched some keys, and the tumult ceased.

Oh thank goodness I can think again. I hope my hearing isn't damaged. Nicholas looks okay too. A security guard? That's who came? Nobody told me there was a security guard. At least he knew what to do. I don't think he's going to arrest us.

"Oh, my goodness, thank you so much," I whined.

"No problem," he said. "It happens all the time."

It happens all the time? I'm not the only dunce who sets off the alarm?

I showed him my instructions. "I followed these directions to the letter. I don't know why it didn't work. Would you know?"

"Like I said, this is not uncommon." He didn't even look at the paper.

"I have to turn the alarm back on when we leave," I said. "Can you walk me through it so it doesn't go off again?"

"Sure." He read the instructions. "Looks pretty straight-forward to me. You shouldn't have any problems."

"Are you sure?" I asked, reading over the directions again.

"If it goes off, I'll just come back," he replied.

So we have to listen to the screeching for another couple of minutes and wait for you again?

"That's great. Thank you again. We really appreciate it."

"Good luck," he said, walking out the door and locking it behind him.

Nicholas and I looked at each other. "Well that was fun!" I exclaimed. "Okay, we have to get to work. Do you know what you're doing today?"

"Yes, Mrs. C said she needs me to put the grommets in the curtain."

"Right. Do you remember how?

"Yes. It's no problem."

"Okay, then. Let's go."

We walked to the auditorium, and there lying on the stage was a blue tarp with a few grommets already installed. Nicholas gathered the tools, and I asked what I could do to help.

As Nicholas worked, I handed him the tools he needed. I felt like a nurse giving the appropriate tools to the surgeon during an operation.

This is some detention. I have to work too! Do some of the teachers here subscribe to the belief that hard work makes you a better person?

As I watched Nicholas work, I thought of the slogan, "Work sets you free" that was posted at the entrance of Auschwitz and other Nazi concentration camps.

That's a depressing thought.

We must have gotten eight or ten grommets done before detention time was over. He was a good worker.

While he was working, I asked him, "What did you do to deserve a detention?"

"I turned on a Bunsen burner."

"Oh. You know that's really dangerous, right?"

"You bet."

"What possessed you to do it?"

"I don't know. Just stupidity, I guess. Sometimes I do things without thinking."

While he was working, we discussed *The Wizard of Oz* production and how his classes were going. He asked if we could turn on the nearby radio. We enjoyed listening to music while we worked. We had a nice system going to get the grommets done. Toward the end of our time together he said, "Ms. B, you're really nice."

"Thank you. You're nice too."

"I didn't know you'd be so nice."

"Well thank you very much."

What did he think I'd be? I guess most kids don't expect any teacher to be nice.

When it was time to leave, I was nervous to reset the alarm.

"Go stand by the door, and I'll make a run for it once the alarm's set. We only have a minute or two to get out of here," I told him.

My hands were shaking as I pushed the buttons.

This was embarrassing enough the first time. I really don't want to go through this again even though this time I know who will come to the rescue.

No ear-blasting siren went off.

"It worked," I said, as I dashed across the lobby toward Nicholas and the door. We pushed the door open and practically fell outside. I slammed the door shut, put the key in the lock and turned it. I withdrew the key, stood there panting, and we waited.

"I think we're good," I said, relieved to hear no sound. "The security man doesn't need to come back."

Just then a car pulled up for Nicholas.

"My ride's here. Bye, Ms. B. Thanks."

"Goodbye," I said waving. Nicholas got in the car, and it pulled away.

I guess his parents don't care to meet me. Oh well. At least this is over. This had to be the worst detention I've ever given. I'll never forget it. I hope I never have another one like it. No one is ever going to talk me into giving a Saturday detention again. After all, who really paid the price for Nicholas's bad behavior— he or I? I think Nicholas actually had a good time. I'm the one who had to suffer through this!

Chapter 11

But deliver us from evil

Richard was excited he was going on a two-week trip to Israel with his buddy, the same one who was there the night we met.

"I had no idea you were planning a trip."

Oh, we started planning it months ago," he said.

"I'll miss you," I told him one night close to his departure as we were eating carryout at his place.

"Oh. ....okay. I'll bring you back something."

"Okay. Thanks."

Oh, okay? Really? Thanks for returning the sentiment. I guess the feelings in this relationship are one way. Maybe he'll feel differently later. I don't care if he brings me back something.

While he was away, I found a box sitting on my doorstep. The return address told me it was from Richard.

Oh wow. He sent me something before he left. He must really like me. I got a present!! Nobody ever sends me anything! This is wonderful.

I brought it in and ripped open the box with my bare hands like Godzilla. I swung open the flaps. Inside the packing peanuts was another small box. The picture on the box was of a camera.

How wonderful! He bought me a brand new camera. He remembered my camera broke and thought to get me a new one. I guess this is my birthday present. I didn't expect a gift. Maybe he really does care for me.

I opened the note. It read, "Happy Birthday. Fondly, Richard."

Fondly? Fondly???! He couldn't even use the word "love"? Is it that hard to write "love"? Writing "love" doesn't mean you are deeply in love. People write it as a way of saying they care. It was thoughtful that he had a birthday present delivered to me while he was away. But "fondly"? He obviously isn't feeling it for me. The note made that very clear. This relationship is doomed.

***

It was Friday a couple weeks before Easter and time again to take the kids to church. We followed Mrs. A's class toward the church, but we walked right past it and out the door.

"Where are we going?" I asked one of Mrs. A's students.

Maybe her class was assigned to do something else, although that's a little strange. Maybe I shouldn't be following them. I wish they'd tell me things. I have a whole class with me and no idea where I'm supposed to be taking them. I feel like Moses leading the Israelites out of Egypt, only we are going to end up in Jordan instead. These kids aren't going to trust me to lead them anywhere ever again. I'm so clueless.

"We are going to church," a boy in Mrs. A's class answered.

"But we just walked past the church."

"We are going to the old church."

"Oh. Okay. Thanks."

I guess they still use the old church. I didn't realize they hold services there. It will be interesting to see what it looks like inside. I've never been in there. I wonder why we are going there instead.

The old church was across the way. As we walked toward it, I noticed old stones at its foundation. It had a shabby wooden exterior that could use a new coat of paint, and the building was obviously older and significantly smaller. I could smell the mildew before we entered the building. We walked up the steps and through the entrance which put us in the back of the church. It was about an eighth of the size of the new church and looked to have been built around the late 1880s.

I can see why they built a new church. Boy, this one's old! I could envision a carriage pulling up providing transport for ladies wearing full-skirted dresses and hats with feathers and brims. "How do you do?" I thought.

The old church was a narrow building with pews on both sides. The pews were a dark, older wood, and the paneling and floor were made of the same wood. The plastered walls were discolored and cracking from age. The altar was at the far end of the room. The whole place reeked.

Boy, they really did need a new church. This one is dank.

We filed into the seats. I ended up in the pew against the far back wall. I had my eighth grade class with me, and I seated myself last as usual. That put me at the end of the pew, seated next to Peter, the charismatic student who had introduced himself to me before school started.

What's in store today? Whatever it is, I'm not going to worry about the service like I usually do. I'm not going to do anything I'm not comfortable with. Although, these services don't seem to require much from the congregants.

The service began, and Peter whispered to me, "Ms. B, today they are doing Stations of the Cross."

Peter is so sweet. He knows he needs to fill me in on what's going on. I didn't even have to ask.

"Huh? What does that mean?"

"It's a different service. They walk the cross around to different stations. It's supposed to be the stations where Jesus stopped on his walk to his crucifixion."

"Oh, wow, okay. Thank you for telling me, Peter."

Say what? We're walking Jesus to be nailed on the cross? Oy vey!! Well this is one of the last places I'd like to be. It's not even a regular service! Besides the fact that Jews don't believe Jesus was the messiah, I'd rather not think about the whole crucifixion. In addition to all its controversy, I am very squeamish. I feel more out of place in this service than in all the other ones I attended. I'll have to sit through this one too.

When the service began, everyone stood, so I joined them. After the pastor said a few words, everyone seated themselves, so again, I followed. Then a cross-bearer flanked by two candle-bearers began walking forward and stopped. Everyone stood again. I wasn't expecting this and must have been daydreaming, because I realized I was still seated. I rose quickly. Peter looked at me and giggled. I smiled and shrugged my shoulders. This reminded me of the game "Simon Says." Only with "Simon Says" you at least get instructions. I was drastically losing this game.

How am I supposed to know this stuff? I'm Jewish! I really have little idea of what is going on much less when to sit and stand. We do a lot of standing and sitting in synagogue, especially during

High Holiday services. But either the Rabbi tells us or the prayer book indicates when we rise and when we sit. Or we just know that you rise when the Ark (containing the Holy Scriptures) is opened. Here there is no clue, yet everyone seems to know what to do. I must be missing something.

After a few more words, everyone sat. Right before everyone sat, Peter tugged on my dress to alert me that we'd be sitting again.

Thank you again, Peter!

After a minute or so, everyone stood again. I arose with a sigh that may have been louder than I intended, because Peter was grinning at me.

The cross-bearer and candle-bearers moved forward. More words were said. When it was time to be seated, Peter signaled me again by leaning his head toward the bench.

What would I do without you, Peter? Thank you for being my savior! So glad someone cares to clue me in so I don't look like too much of a fool!

The service continued in this manner. I listened to the service and understood the routine so that I no longer needed Peter's cues. I wasn't sure what to make of the line where they ask Jesus if he is the king of the Jews and he answers that they tell him he is.

Huh? What kind of an answer is that? What does that mean? They think Jesus is the king of the Jews and nobody says otherwise? Okay, I keep forgetting that supposedly Jesus was Jewish. But king? Huh?

More sitting and more rising ensued. Then they described the physical beating and crucifixion of Jesus, and

I cringed. I looked around, and nobody's face showed much emotion. Hearing this whole story distressed me.

I guess everyone is accustomed to this story, and it doesn't bother them. I suppose it was the Jewish people doing the beating and torturing? Well at least the scripture they are reading doesn't say that, otherwise someone might chase me out of the church. I liked the prayers the pastor was saying about granting us willing spirits and merciful hearts and more. Don't we all pray for those things?

Then I had a disturbing thought.

Were they allowing me to witness this service and others in the hope that I would convert? Do they think that I might change my mind about my own religion? I certainly hope not, because that is not going to happen.

The service ended with a final prayer, and I breathed a sigh of relief. For some reason, this entire service exhausted me. Perhaps it was the constant sitting and standing, or perhaps I was tired from watching Jesus' symbolic journey through the stations. Or perhaps I was just tired from having to attend services that I didn't believe in. Whatever the case, I was happy to lead my students back to class.

As usual, nobody talked to me about the service, although I didn't expect my students to mention it. No teachers asked me what I thought or if I understood what was going on. Perhaps they were afraid I would get into a theological argument or discount everything I had heard. Or perhaps they thought I had no feelings about it at all. Maybe they just didn't care. Never once the entire school year did I have any type of religious discussion with anyone, not even the religion teacher. That was probably a good thing.

***

Shortly after the nightmare PTA meeting where the parent wanted to oust me, Mrs. A notified me that she had a plan.

"Next parent-teacher conferences we're doing together. I'm not leaving you to meet with these parents alone."

I had never thought of doing it together, especially since we didn't teach the same students. I really appreciated that she was thinking of me and protecting me.

She repeated this from time to time. "Remember, we're going to team up and meet these parents together." Or she'd say, "I'm not leaving you to do this by yourself. We are going to have joint conferences." I felt better knowing somebody was in my corner. And I certainly didn't want to face the firing squad alone!

When the day came, I wasn't worried because of her assurances. School was not in session this day, but teachers were present to meet with parents. If the parents were making appointments, they hadn't contacted me directly. All I knew was that conferences were to be no more than thirty minutes. I didn't know whom to expect.

There was breakfast for us in the faculty room. Mrs. A was there getting something and talking with other teachers. I wanted to ask her what our plan was specifically, but there wasn't an opportunity to approach her. Someone made an announcement that it was time to go to our classrooms and start our conferences. The school secretary told me that the Smiths were waiting for me in my classroom. They were the parents of Holly, one of my sixth grade girls.

What? They are already sitting in my classroom? So the appointments are going through the school secretary? Why didn't anyone check with me first? I'm starting with the Smiths? I was certain that they didn't like me and were going to give me a hard time. I wasn't looking forward to facing them. But at least now I had some help.

I didn't see Mrs. A go to her classroom. But when I made it down the hallway, I looked through her window to see her conferencing with a mother, both of them sitting at student desks in the middle of the room, intently involved in conversation.

I was going to politely interrupt and ask if I should join them. I put my hand on the doorknob and turned it. The door wouldn't open. I turned the doorknob the other way, and it still wouldn't open. The door was locked! She had locked me out of her room!

I turned my head and saw the Smiths sitting in my room. I looked through Mrs. A's window again, but she did not turn her head. They continued to have what appeared to be a very in-depth conversation. The parent glanced in my direction but was listening to Mrs. A. I could see the parent didn't say anything to Mrs. A about me being at the door. And Mrs. A never looked up. I removed my hand from the doorknob.

Mrs. A is ignoring me. I'm sure she knows I'm standing here. She must have at least heard the doorknob rattling. I can't believe she did this to me! And the parent sitting there isn't telling her someone is at her door. Did they plan this?

I felt like the victim in a slasher movie. I could feel my eyes "bugging out," the color draining from my face, and my mouth frozen in a long, wide frown. I felt like Michael

Myers, the masked character in the *Halloween* movie, was standing behind me wielding a knife.

Save me!! Don't leave me!!! How can you do this to me?

I wanted to bang on the door, but I didn't want the parent to think I was a maniac or to give Mrs. A the impression that I was helpless and desperate.

I can't believe you actually locked me out. All that talk about how you were going to protect me, and you left me out in the cold and threw me to the wolves! What were you thinking? I know you didn't forget what you said. I can't believe you'd do this to me. What is your problem?

I have nowhere to go. There is no asylum for me anywhere in this school. I can't run to the principal's office, the faculty room, or to someone else's class. I am expected to be in these conferences. The Smiths saw me already, and I have no excuse if I turn around and run away. Nobody else knows what my situation is right now. Nobody is going to help me. I am on a deserted island with little chance of survival. I hope I make it.

I took a deep breath and walked into my classroom.

"Good morning, Mr. and Mrs. Smith. How are you?"

"Fine."

They both sat in the student desks in the front row with their arms crossed.

"Thanks for coming to meet with me."

Mr. Smith grunted.

I grabbed my grade book and my chair from behind my desk and pulled it to sit opposite them.

"Holly is doing very well in my class," I told them. "But you must already know that. Certainly you've seen the graded work come home. Plus, we sent home progress reports several weeks back. You know that she's done very well so far this year. "

"Yes." Their sour, puckered facial expressions showed a distinct distaste of me.

"If we look at her grades for this quarter, she has an A in literature and an A in composition. Did you read the story she wrote recently? It was very good."

"Yes."

I'm just pedaling at this point. I can keep talking about how wonderful their daughter is, but it won't make a difference. They are obviously unhappy, and I'm sure I'm about to hear about it.

"She seems to enjoy the class." I paused, and there was no comment.

I suppose they don't want to admit that Holly actually likes my class. This is reminiscent of the conference with Theresa's mother, but at least these people are not refusing to sit down with me. I guess Mr. and Mrs. Smith don't want their daughter to enjoy being with someone who is Jewish. What else could this be? Maybe I'm jumping to conclusions. Maybe there is something else going on.

I continued. "She has a B in vocabulary. That seems to be more difficult for most of the children. But I'm sure she can raise it to an A by the end of the quarter."

"Uh huh."

"Do you have any concerns? Was there anything in particular you wanted to discuss with me?"

The father spoke while the mother sat in silence. "We don't think you should be teaching in this school."

"Excuse me? What?"

By this point, the comment still took me aback, but after everything I've heard so far this year, I wasn't exactly surprised.

"We believe that only Christian teachers should teach in a Catholic school."

"But I'm teaching English Language Arts."

I'm not going to lose my cool. There's no sense in getting upset, and I certainly don't want them to see that they upset me. Yet I can't believe they came out and said that.

"Doesn't matter. You shouldn't be here."

"I'm not teaching them religion. As a matter of fact, we don't even discuss religion."

"Jewish teachers shouldn't be teaching in a Catholic school. But obviously we've had no say in the matter, so it is what it is."

No sense in arguing with these people. That will only make matters worse. Besides, this is an argument I will never win. I could never change their minds. Even after all my hard work this school year and all I've done for these kids, these people can't appreciate it. All they can see is that I'm Jewish.

And why are they telling me this now? The better part of the school year is over. What's the point of bringing it up? I'm glad I didn't know this before. I don't want to be afraid to say certain things to students because of their parents. I'm glad I didn't know how they feel, although I know others feel this way.

"We'll help her bring her vocabulary grade up," Mrs. Smith said before they left.

Thank goodness they are gone. How many more people are going to march in here and tell me they wish I wasn't here?

I didn't get a breather, as Peter and his father were at my door moments later.

How did the school secretary know that I was done the first conference? I guess they just waited in the hallway. She must send them down in intervals.

They came in and sat down in the same seats previously occupied by the Smiths. Peter looked like his usual laid back, easy-going self, so I assumed his father would be the same. Instead, I could see that his father was tense and unhappy. He glared at me with piercing, narrowed eyes and a clenched mouth.

I felt bad for this particular family because earlier in the school year the mother passed away. Peter was one of five. He was the one with the twin brother in Mrs. A's class, and his younger sister was in my seventh grade class. Their mother had lost a long battle to cancer, and when it was nearing the end, the kids missed school to be with her. Peter's mother was well-known and well-respected, and many of the teachers had attended the funeral. Mrs. A had placed a special photo of her with a caption in the school yearbook.

The kids had, of course, missed even more school when she died. My heart hurt for them. Even though I never met Peter's parents before, I thought his father looked like he aged more than he should have. He couldn't have been more than forty-something, but he had deep wrinkles, and his hair was turning gray. I expected him to be relatively kind since I always found Peter to be very compassionate and friendly. Plus, I thought that having lost his wife, he would be somewhat amenable. I could see before he spoke how wrong I was.

"How is my son doing exactly?" Peter's father barked at me.

Wow. Let's do away with any niceties, shall we?

"I'm sure Peter can tell you himself. Peter, why don't you give your father an update?"

"Don't ask him. I'm talking to you. You tell me how he's doing."

Holy crap. Here goes another wonderful conference. I guess I'm going to have to answer the man.

"Peter's grades are just fine. But I'd like to talk to you alone. Can we ask Peter to go wait in the lobby or somewhere?"

"No. Anything you have to say, you can say to both of us."

Boy, he is making this really difficult. I don't want Peter to hear me talk about how I think his mother's death has affected him. And I don't think he needs to hear what I think about some of his behavior. Well, now, I have no choice, so I'll just have to choose my words carefully.

"Peter's grades are fine. I'm more worried about his behavior. While it is wonderful how he participates in class and is often enthusiastic, sometimes he speaks out of turn and is a little too loud."

"Yes, I'm sorry, Ms. B. I know I've been rude lately. I promise I'll do better about that," Peter interjected before his father could speak.

"Thank you, Peter. I appreciate that."

His father didn't respond.

Thank goodness Peter admitted that. I don't want another argument on my hands today.

"Was there anything else I need to know?" Peter's father asked.

"No, that's all there is."

"Come on, Peter. Let's go." They disappeared.

What a shame his dad was so curt. I hope he is nice to his children. They need to be comforting each other at this time in their lives. And sometimes teachers need to make exceptions for students with special circumstances, which is why I let Peter get away with some behavior. I'm glad now that I didn't give him some detentions I felt he deserved. I wouldn't want to deal with his father over it!

***

Mrs. Wheeler had scheduled a conference with me some time before the official parent-teacher conferences took place. She had written me a note that she wanted to meet because her son's grades had dropped. She didn't think my grades were justified. I could tell from the note she was peeved. I was glad she scheduled a conference, because she needed to be informed of her son's laziness and lackadaisical attitude. The child hadn't cared much about doing anything the last month or so. I had checked with his other teachers, and they said his grades and effort were mediocre in their classes.

Mr. Z informed me that I'd be meeting her in his office during my planning period.

I had no choice but to agree to that.

I guess she decided to go over my head to the principal before I had a chance to respond to her note. That wasn't very nice. If we have to meet in Mr. Z's office, this has the potential to be really bad. We have another angry parent, and this time we need mediation. I can tell from her note that she blames me for Charlie's poor grades. But I'm not the one to blame. It's her son's fault. He's been a pretty poor student of late. I had my notes and grades to prove it.

Mrs. Wheeler and her son were seated on the principal's black leather sofa when I arrived. Mr. Z was behind his desk on the phone.

Charlie is joining us for this meeting? Well, okay. I guess that can work. I just wish someone would have warned me.

Mr. Z put the phone down and stood up. "Excuse me. I have to take care of something. I'll be right back. Please start without me."

I watched him leave the room.

Oh no! Please don't leave me alone in here with them. I know neither of them likes me. I don't want to be subjected to more nastiness, and I don't want to have to defend myself.

"Hello, Mrs. Wheeler," I said.

"Good morning." She had a sourpuss look on her face. Her son sat there with his arms crossed.

"Thank you for meeting with me," I said.

"Yes. I'd like to know why Charlie is receiving these grades. I know he's been doing his homework. And his grades have never been this low before. I'm very concerned."

"Actually, I'm concerned as well."

The principal walked back into his office and sat down, giving us his full attention.

Oh, he's back. Is that good or bad? Now I think that I'd rather do this in private instead of having him judging me, interrupting me, or even perhaps taking over and not letting me handle this myself. Although I suppose it is good to have a witness. Will he support me if I need it?

156

I continued. "You are correct that his grades have dropped substantially. As I said before, I'm worried about him too."

I need to repeat myself for the principal.

"He definitely isn't putting forth much effort into any of the work he does in class."

Her sourpuss face became replaced with anger as she looked toward her son.

"Charlie, is this true? Are you not trying?"

This is interesting. She must know he's not trying to do well for her to ask. I wonder if there's something they're not telling me. Perhaps she shared something with Mr. Z. beforehand.

"I'm doing my work," Charlie answered sheepishly. "I do everything she tells me to do."

That child is going to sit here and lie in front of all of us. Unbelievable. He thinks he's going to get away with this.

I opened the loose leaf binder I brought with me.

"This is the record I keep of the books each student reads on their own. I go around before reading time, and each student calls out the title of the book they are reading. Here is Charlie's list."

I held it up.

"He has been reading *The Kid Who Only Hit Homers* for almost 2 months now. It's not that big of a novel, and I can count eight weeks that he's telling me he's reading the same book. I asked him to move to a new book weeks ago, and he has not."

"Charlie.....," Mrs. Weaver looked livid by this point.

"Also, I've been having the kids choose which grammar exercise they want to do in the textbook depending upon what they need to know for their own writing. I've discussed with each child what they need to work on. Charlie has completed the exercise for using commas with conjunctions three times already. I asked him to work on something a little more difficult, but he insists that he needs to work on commas. I think he knows how to use a comma with a conjunction by now. I've seen him use it in his own writing."

"Charlie...really?!" Charlie was actually smiling.

"Well, that's what I felt like working on."

"Charlie!!!"

Look at that! His true personality is coming out. They can see he thinks this is funny. This is the same attitude he's had in class, seemingly mocking me and making fun of the entire learning process. Now it's obvious he doesn't take this seriously.

"Thank you, Ms. B. Charlie and I will continue this conversation at home."

She arose and Charlie followed.

"Thank you, Mr. Z," she said as they headed out of the office.

This went better than I expected. At least the woman believed me, and thank goodness I had proof. Thank goodness I write notes. I hope this helps and Charlie actually improves. I know he can do much better. Part of the problem is that he is such a smart aleck. I'm sure his parents must know. Charlie looked so smug at the beginning, as if he thought he could get away with doing hardly anything in my class. Why would he have thought that? Well I hope that Charlie actually buckles down and gets to work. That kid has a lot of potential. I don't know if it helped that we were in the principal's office. At least this time I didn't have to take the blame for something going badly.

Chapter 12

For thine is the kingdom

During spring break (called Easter break by everyone else), I spent Passover with my family. We all live locally, so I didn't have to travel. We had our Seders on the first two nights of Passover, as is the custom. I always enjoy Seder, because there is a structured order to the service read right at the dinner table which leads up to a meal and continues for a short while after, ending with festive singing. ("Seder" means "order.") I like to hear the retelling of the Exodus story where the Jews fled Egypt.

As a child, it is just a bible story, but for me, the stories became more meaningful into adulthood as my understanding grew. Many of the stories we read throughout the year tell of the Jews fleeing persecution, and I felt like I too was a Jew in a foreign land facing similar ignorance, oppression and ill-treatment. I was especially glad to celebrate a Jewish holiday instead of a Catholic one. I never liked matzah, nor any of the foods made with matzah that we are required to eat for the eight days of Passover. The holiday mandates that we not eat any kind of leavened bread, since when the Jews were in the desert, they had no time for their bread to rise. I also never liked chopped liver or gefilte fish, which are traditional Jewish foods also eaten on this holiday.

When we returned to school, some students asked me if I had a nice Passover, and I said I did. That was the extent of the conversation. They didn't ask me any specifics. Perhaps their parents warned them against having any conversations with me about religion, or maybe they just weren't interested. I certainly knew by now not to elaborate on anything Jewish. I did have a nice vacation, as I was always happy to have a break from work although I never called it work; I always said I was going to school, or I had school work to do.

***

One day after Spring break while my seventh grade class was working quietly, I ducked into my closet. It was really just an excuse to be by myself for a moment, although I was sure to reappear with papers in hand so it didn't look suspicious. I went into the closet and closed the door, standing there for a few minutes silently sobbing. I couldn't let the kids hear me. Thankfully no students asked for me during that time. I didn't hear any voices, and no hands were raised when I emerged. Before I reappeared, I wiped my eyes with my sleeve and hoped nobody would notice my tear-stained face. I wasn't sure exactly how I looked, since there was no mirror in the closet. Nobody said anything. Kids are the first to point something out, so nobody noticed. I did this on and off for a week or more. I was glad I had a walk-in closet, because there was no bathroom nearby and I couldn't leave my class.

Richard had broken up with me, and I was devastated. It was right after he returned from his trip to Israel. I was over his house, and he was distant and quiet.

"Is everything okay?" I asked.

"No, not really," he responded.

"What's wrong?"

"Well, while I was away, I had an epiphany. I was standing at the Western Wall, and I realized that we aren't right for each other. We just don't work."

He had to stand at the Western Wall to have an epiphany? He came to this conclusion all the way on the other side of the world?

"What? We don't work?"

"You and I just weren't meant to be together."

"Oh.....are you sure?"

"Yes, I'm certain."

"So then we are breaking up?"

"Yes."

"Well okay then." I had no argument. I didn't want to have him change his mind and then decide this again like the last time. Besides, I expected this.

I left rather hurriedly. I cried the whole way home. I cried in my apartment. I cried on the phone to my parents, and I cried intermittently in my classroom closet. I felt unlovable and lonely. I was reeling from the fact that I had been dumped. I was floundering like a fish on the end of a fishing hook; I didn't know where to go or what to do with myself. I certainly didn't feel like going to school, but I didn't have a choice, so I forced myself. I forced myself to get out of bed in the morning. I forced myself to eat. I forced myself to get in the car and drive to school. I was like that same fish, moving my fins with an involuntary motion, hoping to be put back in the water, but I knew I wasn't going back and that he'd never call me again. I hurt so much that I felt like I had been gutted. I walked around feeling empty inside for a long time. Seeing my students would cheer me up and distract me at least.

My mother said to me, "There are lots of fish in the sea," but I didn't feel like I'd ever catch the right one. I felt as if I had been thrown back. As with most break-ups, as time went on, I slowly started to feel better and make fewer trips to my walk-in closet. There would be more boyfriends and more breakups in my future.

***

Springtime seemed like the right time for a fun unit that would get the kids on their feet and lift my spirits as well. It was time for Drama! While I worked on specific plays with my sixth and seventh graders, my eighth graders begged me to let them write an original play. Several of them already had an idea for a plot, and the rest of the kids in the class agreed to be in the play. After much pleading, mostly by very vocal Peter, I consented.

The kids wrote an entire play about a drug lord and his gang. I told them we needed to work on it together. While I appreciated and admired all their hard work, the script was lacking. They begged me to let them start to work on the scenery anyway, and again I acquiesced, because I needed time to figure out how we could fix this script. So for a couple of days, they painted a scene of Washington, DC on a large white sheet.

I took that weekend to think about their play. I was wishing I had some help. I had no clue how to fix it. It read like a bad 1930s script about the mafia. There was no great plot or resolution. The characters were totally unrelatable and a far cry from any real person they had ever come in contact with. I had no idea how to make it work and still use their ideas. After all these weeks, I couldn't tell them to scrap the whole thing. I figured we'd have a development meeting and discuss the problem. Maybe we could figure it out together.

We never had the meeting. Once again Mrs. A came into my room during our planning period with some earth-shaking, plan-changing, unexpected news. By now you'd think I'd realize how much she must have enjoyed upending all my plans.

"Diane, I forgot to tell you that every year we have an oratorical contest for the eighth grade, and the winner gets a prize."

"What? Oh. What does that mean exactly?"

"The lady who donates the prize money comes into school and judges all the speeches."

"So what are you saying? The end of the year is about eight weeks away."

"Yes. And the contest is in two weeks."

"What? Two weeks?"

"Yes. Your class should be working on their speeches. I meant to tell you before."

"So you're saying we need to stop what we're doing?"

"Yes, right now."

"But we're in the middle of our drama unit, and the eighth graders wrote a play."

"Well, you'll have to stop and have them start their speeches. There's no time to waste."

"What are they supposed to write and speak about?"

"They are to write about how someone was the most influential person in their lives."

"Oh."

"It can be anybody they choose. Most kids write about their parents."

"Oh."

"Good luck." She just about skipped out of the room.

Oh no! Now I have to change everything. I need to make new plans. This is no small feat. We only have two weeks?! I have to walk them through the whole writing process before we can even begin the speaking part. And then I have to teach them how to speak in public. I don't think any of them have ever spoken in front of a crowd before. They are coming in next period. We need to start this now.

When the class came in, I broke the news to them.

"So unfortunately we need to abandon the play. I'm sorry. I know how much this meant to all of you."

"That's okay, Ms. B. It's not your fault," Peter said.

"Yeah, we can use the script another time," Colin chimed in.

I love these kids.

"Then let's start the speeches. Do you all know what the assignment is?"

"Yeah, my sister did it years ago," Mary Ann said. "We have to speak about an important person in our lives."

164

Years ago? I bet they had this same contest when the school was first built.

"Correct. So why don't we do some brainstorming independently?"

Douglas raised his hand. "Yes, Douglas?"

"I already know who I'm writing about."

"So do I," Jennifer exclaimed.

"Do you all know?"

"Yes!" they all cried out.

I wanted to make sure no one was undecided.

"Raise your hand if you have already decided whom you are writing about."

All hands were raised.

Wow. They probably saw this coming and were already planning on it.

"So do we need to do any prewriting?"

"I don't," Douglas said.

"Neither do I," Talia agreed.

"Well, those who are ready to write may certainly do so. Those who need to work on their ideas, should do some prewriting first. You can let me know what you need."

The students went right to work. They worked very hard for two weeks and were ready to deliver their speeches on time. I was proud of them. Once their final drafts were complete, we practiced giving these speeches one by one for several days. We worked on eye contact, intonation, speed, calming our nerves, and every other skill necessary to deliver a fine speech. All twelve of them had a well-written speech which they delivered nicely.

Peter was the only student to write a speech but not

deliver it. He approached me in the parking lot at recess one day and told me he couldn't do it.

"Why not?" I asked.

"I wrote about my mother."

"Oh. Wow. Okay....What do you want to do?"

"I can't read this to everyone."

"I completely understand. I don't know what you've written. Do you want to read it to just me right now?"

"Okay."

He started to read his speech. Two lines into it, I was tearing up. At about the second paragraph, he started choking up and couldn't speak.

"Okay. That's fine, Peter," I said. "You don't need to read anymore. Look, you have me crying too!"

I gave him a hug. I looked toward the front door of the school, and I could have sworn I saw the principal standing by the door watching us. Perhaps it was my imagination, but I had a feeling he was wondering why I was hugging Peter. Poor kid had lost his mother, and I couldn't just let him stand there crying.

"Why don't you go inside and ask Mr. Z what he wants us to do since he knows the situation?"

"Okay."

He walked across the parking lot and into the school. I thought I saw Mr. Z open the door for him. I found out later that Mr. Z had Peter read the speech to only him. Peter told me he had a hard time getting through it, but he was able to make it to the end. I was glad Mr. Z showed compassion. I could never see Peter delivering that speech in front of the whole school.

When the day came for the speeches, chairs were set up on the gymnasium floor and the podium was placed onstage. Mrs. A, Mr. Z, and a flock of people escorted the sponsor. They reminded me of Emperor penguins huddled in Antartica, moving together in one direction to keep warm. It took several minutes for them to get the woman to her seat. Between all the people surrounding her, I caught a glimpse of a diminutive older lady walking with a cane. Mrs. A had told me that she donates a lot of money to the school and expects to be treated royally when she comes. It looked as if everyone was "kissing up to her," especially Mrs. A, who was interminably by her side and talking incessantly. Mrs. A, Mr. Z, and the little old lady sat together in the first row. I was seated a few rows behind and was never introduced. The entire school came to hear the speeches except for the youngest grades. A few parents were present. I was nervous for my students.

We sat through two hours of speeches. I listened intently to each one. I knew my kids' speeches pretty well, so I really wanted to listen to those of Mrs. A's students. I was certainly comparing their speeches to ours. I was proud that my students' speeches were just as good even though I had the "lesser ability" class and less time to prepare. The kids spoke about parents, older siblings, grandparents and other family members, teachers, celebrities, and famous people. I was jealous when one student spoke about her favorite teacher who had retired from this school. I was wondering if I was worthy enough to have any student use me as the subject of his or her speech. I aspired to be that kind of teacher.

My favorite speech was from Mrs. A's student who

spoke about her grandfather who had survived the Korean War. I thought it was the most powerful speech of the day, and I could relate since my father had been through a war. I was particularly touched by how she mentioned the action he saw and explained the qualities that made him a hero. But this orator didn't win or even place in the contest. I was surprised. I was wondering what was going through the mind of this little old lady and what exactly she was looking for. Mrs. A had told me that her husband had passed away, and the money she donated for the contest was in his honor. What pertinent information did Mrs. A exclude when she glossed over the requirements of this contest?

After all the speeches were read, there was a fifteen-minute break. Mrs. A disappeared with the benefactor. When they returned, the first, second and third place winners were announced. A girl from Mrs. A's class won first place. I was not surprised, as her class had the advantage. Who knows how early Mrs. A started her class on the assignment without notifying me. Second place was taken by a boy in Mrs. A's class. Happily, one of my students came in third. Hooray! We had a victory after all our hard work. I was thinking that Mrs. A made sure one of my students won something so it wouldn't look rigged.

After the winners were announced and awards handed out, Mrs. A and Mr. Z had their photograph taken with the benefactor and the winners. Parents were snapping pictures. Mrs. A and Mr. Z were having their pictures taken with students. By then it was time for dismissal. No one asked me to be in a photo. I played up our win the following day at school and made sure my students knew how proud I was of them.

Chapter 13

the power and the glory

It was the night of the big show, the school's production of *The Wizard of Oz*. It was a Friday night, and I was tired and feeling like I was coming down with a virus. I wanted to go home to bed. I was sick several times throughout the school year. My body wasn't accustomed to being attacked by so many children's germs all day long. It was fighting an invisible war. They say teachers build immunity, but for me it hadn't happened. Several students asked me to come to the show, and I couldn't say no. I went home and dragged myself back to see it.

I was trying to find a seat in the gymnasium, thinking that at least I could sit down for a while. I looked around for a seat, avoiding any seats next to parents. My behind was almost in a chair when I heard, "Ms. B! Ms. B! We need you!"

Cassidy ran over to me and began pulling me with her. "Laura needs you," she pleaded, leading me backstage. Laura was sitting on the backstage steps with her glasses in her hand.

"Ms. B, can you hold these for me?" she asked, extending them to me.

"Okay, sure," I said, wondering why this was such an urgent matter. I turned to walk back to my seat.

"No! You can't leave. I need them as soon as I get off the stage, or I can't see where I'm going. And I need to change costumes for the next scene."

"Okay. Well what do you want me to do?"

"Can you just stand here and hold my glasses?" she whined.

"Isn't there somewhere you can put them where you can retrieve them later?"

"No. Please....I need you to just stay here and hold them."

"Well....uh...okay..."

Again, I couldn't say no. I stayed in that one spot throughout her performances, holding her eyeglasses and handing them to her when needed. I was so tired that I sat myself on the steps and hoped no one would trip over me. Actors rushed past me as they exited off the stage, and I flattened myself as close to the wall as possible.

I can't injure an actor and be responsible for the collapse of this show. So much for enjoying the show from my own seat.

How do I get myself into these things? Surely there must be somewhere to put these darn glasses! Rats, I don't see one single place. I'm stuck doing this. I feel so out-of-place. At least I have an interesting perspective to watch the show. Although I'm sure the view from the audience is better. This isn't very much fun.

Once the show was over, I realized I never saw the curtain Nicholas and I grommeted during his detention on that infamous alarm-ringing Saturday. I wondered if it ever got used or if it was just an exercise in futility.

I was thrilled, of course, when Laura didn't need me anymore. It was intermission, and I must have sat there on those steps for over an hour. I was feeling so poorly by this time that I decided to leave. I exited the gymnasium just as the lights lowered and the second half began.

Monica stopped me in the lobby to chat. She reentered the gymnasium to catch the rest of the show, and the doors closed behind her. I was headed for the main exit when the Tin Man, the Scarecrow, and the Cowardly Lion appeared, standing in front of the gymnasium doors, jiggling the doorknob.

"Ms. B, we need help. We can't get back on stage. The doors are locked."

"What? Are you serious?"

I jiggled the door handle myself as if only I possessed the power to open it like I was the Wizard of Oz himself. Sure enough, they wouldn't open. Nobody could hear a knock over the noise inside, and we knew nobody was near the door. I jiggled the door handle again and wrapped on the door for a few times anyway, hoping somebody with exceptional hearing would answer.

"What should we do?" the Cowardly Lion implored. "We're on stage in a minute." Ironically, he seemed to be shaking all over, staying within character.

"You'll have to use the other door. I don't have time to run around and open this door for you."

"We'll end up approaching from the other end of the stage," the tin man squeaked. No oil would help fix this problem. Only perhaps a key would.

"Which is better—to show up on the wrong side or to not show up at all?" I asked them.

I expected the scarecrow to cross his arms in front of his chest and point in both directions saying, "Let's go this way."

Instead they muttered "okay," and rushed past me, rounding the corner, and making their cue on time. I could hear from behind the locked doors that the audience wasn't booing or complaining, so everything was okay. They told me on Monday that it was fine. The actors and crew were a little confused when they appeared stage left instead of stage right, but the show went on. I had to laugh to myself, as I could envision the Wizard and his cronies craning their necks, shielding their eyes with their hands, and searching dramatically in one direction while the characters appeared from another. I never asked what they were doing outside the doors in the first place or why the doors would be locked. What a production when the main actors can't get back on stage!

I made sure to tell the students that their performances were wonderful. I was surprised at how these children acted like professionals and really embraced their parts. I suppose they had good coaching, as the science teacher was a very patient woman who could get the best out of people. The girl who played Dorothy could really sing. She was a fifth grader I didn't know. Parent volunteers had helped with the costumes and scenery and did a fantastic job. I was impressed with the background paintings of Emerald City and the munchkin village. I felt bad that I hadn't helped much with the production, but I was exhausted as it was.

I was headed to the front door again when I decided that I might as well stay and watch the rest of the show since it was almost over. I walked around to the unlocked set of doors and stood in the back of the gymnasium since it was too much trouble to find a seat. When the show ended, everyone applauded and hooted, but there was no standing ovation. I was disappointed for the kids.

The gymnasium emptied out quickly. Parents took their kids home right away. I was surprised there weren't a whole lot of congratulatory conversations and bouquets of flowers. I remembered some papers I forgot to take home earlier and walked back to my room. I was glad I remembered, or my kids would have to wait a couple more days to get an assignment returned.

When I returned to the lobby, it was empty except for the social studies and math teachers, the gregarious duo. The social studies teacher had told Joseph that he may have gotten out of serving a detention with me (over not coming to class with a writing utensil), but he was not going to get out of serving any detentions with her. She voluntarily gave me a National Geographic magazine article on Pompeii when my sixth graders read a story about it. When we read *The Phantom Tollbooth*, the math teacher had given me a sheet where kids could make their own dodecahedrons since that was a character in the story. She was also the one who took my hand during that first teacher church service. I felt like these ladies were on my side.

I walked to the front door and stopped. Looking through the large plate-glass windows, I saw an empty parking lot shrouded in darkness. There was not one flood light or landscape light illuminating one square inch of that parking lot. It was fodder for any criminal on the loose or in hiding. There must have been a lunar eclipse.

The science and math teachers also stopped when they saw the darkness.

"Oh, it's really dark out there," the social studies teacher observed.

"We'll walk out with you, Diane," the math teacher said comfortingly.

Thank goodness, because I don't want to go out there by myself. That just looks scary. I feel like a sitting duck for any prowler, pervert or convict. Anyone could come along and whisk me away sight unseen. Come Monday morning, someone might notice I wasn't in class.

A parent appeared in the lobby, and they started conversing. The talking went on and on. I shifted my weight and moved my bag to the other shoulder. I stared at them, but they were looking at each other, so I stared out the window.

How long is this going to take? I can't wait here much longer. They know I'm waiting to leave. They said they'd walk out with me. They could at least tell me they didn't forget about me—that I should wait or that I should leave without them. Are they doing this on purpose? I thought they were my friends or at least supportive of me. I guess I was wrong. They obviously are not going to walk out with me. Maybe they think this is funny. I'm abandoned again.

After a full five minutes, I put my hand on the door to walk out by myself.

"Ms. B, we'll walk out with you," I heard from behind me.

Thank goodness, whoever it is.

I turned around to find Peter, his twin brother, and his younger sister, Brianna.

"We'll walk out together. It's really dark out there," Peter said.

They walked me to my car, chatting about the show and thanking me for helping with the locked door debacle, since they heard about it.

These are the sweetest kids. There are two adults in there who left me hanging out to dry, but here are three kids that are making sure I get to my car. I hope these kids never change.

"How are you getting home?" I asked, all of a sudden realizing that I hadn't thought about them.

"Our ride is over there," Brianna said, pointing to a car idling in the back of the parking lot. "See you Monday!" Peter shouted as they sprinted toward it.

"See you Monday."

I drove home thinking about Peter's performance. He had played Toto in a full-length furry dog costume. He was stooping throughout the show, down on all fours. He never complained about being the dog. As a matter of fact, the science teacher told me he asked for the part. She was going to use a stuffed animal, but Peter begged her to let him do it. She said that it must have been very hot in that costume. I thought about how his legs must be hurting and how amazing it was that he could perform like that.

These kids are amazing. They are going to grow up and be important people in this world one day. I hope I get to see it.

175

***

For our sixth grade drama unit, we read the play, *The Phantom Tollbooth*, by Norton Juster. This is a novel and a play about a young boy named Milo who drives his electric car through a tollbooth he builds from a kit and enters a foreign land filled with fantastical creatures and places, such as Dictionopolis , Digitoplis and the Land of Ignorance. Since the sixth graders weren't required to give speeches, we were able to actually complete this unit. During this unit they wrote some dialogue and parts of a script, drew and analyzed characters and settings, and examined the language of the play. The children were so insightful that some of their comments really impressed me, such as when Kathleen said, "Milo's biggest obstacle is himself," and Nadine said, "The pencil is valuable because Milo will be able to solve problems himself that come up in life." My students' critical thinking and reading skills were really sharp! And they call them lower-ability kids!

For final projects, I asked the students to form groups and act out scenes from the play. I let them choose, so some groups performed the same scenes. Needless to say, the performances were adorable because my students were very creative and imaginative. It helped that they were using a well-written play that provided a wealth of material. I required students to wear costumes and bring props. I was impressed that some students had memorized their lines and some had even improvised!

Billy played the whether man (who discusses whether or not there is any weather) and used an umbrella. One of the groups put chairs together and pretended that it was Milo's car while the other kids in the group provided the car's sound effects. Some of the kids were convincing as lethargarians, drowsy creatures who do nothing but fall asleep at any given moment. They would yawn repeatedly and collapse on the floor, pretending to snooze. They were making me sleepy! James played the watchdog, Tock (a dog with a clock as part of his body), and did a great job making ticking noises and running around on all fours much like Peter did in *The Wizard of Oz*.

When our drama unit was over, it was May. But I was going to squeeze in one more unit before the end of the year, "The Novel." We still had an entire novel to read, and I knew we could finish it. While I was happy that the school year was almost over and I was going to get a vacation from working around the clock, I was going to miss my students. I also was upset because there were so many more things I wanted to do with them!

Chapter 14

forever and ever

There were only a few weeks of school remaining, and I felt there'd be no resolution to the nasty note incident from the first day of school. I figured I would have to let it go. What else could I do? Making a big stink about it wouldn't help the situation. Perhaps the administration (a.k.a. the principal) knew who it was and was protecting him or her for some reason. It was feeling like a giant cover-up. Perhaps revealing the perpetrator would acknowledge the indecent behavior of some parents, and nobody wanted to do that. I was just glad I survived the school year, and I was still teaching.

It was dismissal one day at the beginning of June, and the fifth grade teacher next door sent a student over to my room.

"Mrs. F wants to see you as soon as you can come over," the child urgently instructed. I had found Mrs. F to be a pleasant woman. She had two young children and was always friendly. She had taught quite a few of my students the previous year, so before school started, she filled me in on what I should know about some kids. I was very grateful.

I was busy getting kids ready to leave. As soon as my classroom was empty, I walked up the small set of steps and to her door. She still had a group of students in her room, but she came out into the hallway.

She whispered, "Diane, one of my students told me that she overheard my homeroom student, Jane, talking to another girl about how her older brother was bragging to someone about what he did to a teacher. This is Jane, the younger sister of your eighth grade student, Greg. I think this might be the break you've been looking for. If I were you, I'd talk to Greg right away."

"Oh. Okay."

I had to let this all sink in. *Who was talking to whom? They said what? Jane was talking about her older brother? Greg? Greg is the one I've been looking for? Greg is the culprit?! Really? I wouldn't have guessed. He never showed any signs of hate or prejudice. He and I always seem to get along.*

I must have stood dumbfounded for too long, because Mrs. F repeated herself.

"Diane, you'll talk to Greg, right?"

"Oh, yes. Thank you so much. I'm so glad you told me."

I went home that night thinking how I was going to handle this situation. Greg and I would have a nice, long sit-down. I wasn't sure when I could get him for one though. I didn't want to keep him after school. It would have been too much trouble to deal with transportation and explain why I was detaining him. I didn't want it to feel like a detention at this point.

The solution to that problem was dropped right in my

lap. The religion teacher came to my doorway.

"Diane, I heard that Greg is the one who left that note on your desk the first day of school. You are welcome to take him out of my class to talk to him. Actually, I think you should. It's very appropriate for you to pull him out of religion class for this. He has religion class the same time you have your free period. Would you like me to send him to you?"

"Sure. That would be good. Thanks so much."

How did she know already? I still can't get over how fast word travels around here. I guess everyone knows. Even so, I haven't heard anything from Mrs. A or the principal about it. Surely they've heard.

I hope nobody says anything to Greg before I can talk to him. I guess there are no consequences for his actions except however I choose to handle it. Apparently nobody else is going to do anything. There's no sense in giving him a detention. What's the point of giving one or even several detentions for an infraction of this magnitude? What possible consequence would even be appropriate for something of this nature? How can I teach him the seriousness and consequences of his actions? Besides, he got away with it the entire school year. I just need to talk to him and clear the air. I need to find out what he was thinking and if he still feels the same way, because that's the important thing.

The social studies teacher dropped by my room the next day. She came over to my desk where I was sitting grading papers during my planning period.

"What are you going to say to Greg?" she asked me.

"What?"

"What are you going to say to Greg when you talk to him about what he did?"

Holy cow. My life's an open book here. Apparently everybody knows. Who else is going to drop by and ask me about it? Why does she even want to know? I'm not going to bother to ask her how she found out or why she is asking. I don't want to get into that.

"Oh, I figured we'd just talk about what happened and I'd include some history of anti-Semitism," I answered.

"Oh. Which history were you thinking?"

"The Holocaust, Hitler, etc." I told her.

"That sounds good. Don't forget the Spanish Inquisition," she said walking toward the door. "That was important too."

"Oh, okay."

The Spanish Inquisition? I don't remember anything about the Spanish Inquisition. What does that matter? I just need to get my point across. I'm not interested in a full history lesson. Is that all she cares about? How about if he feels any remorse for what he did? How about if he learned anything about accepting people of other faiths, nationalities, cultures and religions? Why don't we care about that?

About a week before the last day of school, Greg appeared as scheduled in my room during my planning period. I figured it worked out this way for a reason. We were meant to have this conversation. It was already a hot, summer day, and the school had no air-conditioning. I was having yet another important conversation in uncomfortable school surroundings. But at least this time I was smart enough to not wear panty hose.

"Yes, Ms. B, you wanted to see me?" Greg asked from my doorway.

"Come in and have a seat, Greg," I directed, pointing to the chair next to my desk. I pulled my desk chair out to sit beside him.

Surely he must have an idea about why I called him into my room when he has another class. I know he remembers what he did.

"I don't suppose you have any idea why I asked to see you today?"

"No, Ms. B."

"Is there anything you think you should tell me? Anything we should talk about?"

"Not that I can think of."

"Are you sure? Is there anything you've done that you think we should discuss?"

"No, Ms. B."

"Anything at all from any time during the school year?"

"No, Ms. B."

Is he kidding me? How can he pretend he hasn't done anything? I'm pretty sure this is the right kid. I don't think there's a mistake. Is it possible he has forgotten?

I decided to be more direct.

"I heard you were the one who left that note on my desk the first day of school."

"Oh, no, Ms. B. That wasn't me."

He knows exactly what note I mean. He's not even asking me what I'm talking about.

"It wasn't you?"

"Oh, no. It wasn't me," he replied, shaking his head.

"Really, because I know it was your handwriting."

Oh my gosh. It most certainly was his handwriting. Eureka! I could see that now. Even after all the work I received from him throughout the school year, I hadn't realized it. I wasn't looking. I had chosen to put the incident aside and not do a handwriting analysis of each student. I didn't have time for that anyway. And I couldn't have tried to match it up if I wanted to, since I never got the index card back. But I do remember

182

what it looked like, and I'm pretty sure that was Greg's handwriting!

Mrs. A had known it all along. She recognized his handwriting when she saw that note the very first time and scrunched up her face. She had taught him the year before, and she knew it was him. Yet she had said nothing. I was sure of it.

"It wasn't me," Greg repeated.

"Really? Then who was it?"

"It was Nicholas. He did it."

Aha! I've got a name!

"Nicholas? Mrs. A's student?"

"Yes, him."

"Hmmm....that's interesting."

I was thinking back to the time I served Nicholas Saturday detention. Again, I never would have guessed he had anything to do with it either. He was a likeable fellow, and we had pleasant conversations. I had no idea he harbored any anti-Semitic feelings. How could I have known?

"It was all Nicholas's idea." My silence had made him even more uncomfortable.

The truth is slowly coming to light. I'm finally getting to the bottom of this.

"Really?"

"Yes. He came to me and told me what he was going to do."

"He did? And what did he say? What did you say?"

"He said it was a joke."

"What did you say? Did you think it was a joke?"

"No."

"Then why didn't you tell him not to do it? Why didn't you tell him it sounded like a bad idea?"

"I don't know."

"Hmmmm."

"Well, ...actually....I did think it was a joke."

"Oh, I see."

"But I know now that it wasn't a joke."

"How so?"

"I see that it wasn't funny."

After another moment of silence, Greg said, "Actually he forced me to write the note."

"Really?"

Now we've gone from not doing it but knowing about it to being the one who did it.

"He pressured me into doing it."

"How so?"

"Well....I said I'd do it. I was just going along with him."

"So you wanted to do it?"

"Actually, I thought it was funny too, at the time."

"So you were an accomplice."

"Yes, I guess so."

"You know that an accomplice is just as guilty, right? In a real crime, accomplices go to jail too."

"Yes."

"Was anyone else involved? Did anyone influence Nicholas or you to do it in the first place? Was there an adult or another person who conspired in this?"

"No."

"Nobody else said anything to influence you or Nicholas to write the note?"

"No, no one."

"So then you're telling me Nicholas came up with this

idea himself?"

"Yes."

"So what were you thinking? You really thought it was funny? Did you realize how serious this is?"

"Yes, I'm sorry. I feel really bad about it." He was looking down at the floor.

"Do you understand what it all means?"

"Yes."

"Tell me what it all means."

"Well, we thought at the time it was funny, giving a new teacher a hard time when she started a new school."

"Do you understand why it's not funny? Do you understand what you wrote?"

"Yes."

"Tell me, please."

"It's not funny to make fun of someone's religion."

"Yes. That's true. Would you like someone to make fun of your belief in Catholicism or anything else for that matter? How would it make you feel if you received a note saying that you were wrong to believe in Jesus?"

"Pretty bad."

"Right. How do you think your note made me feel?"

"Pretty bad. I know it hurt your feelings."

"Yes, it did. And I had to go through the entire school year teaching in spite of that nasty note. "

"I'm sorry."

"I always thought you and I had a good relationship," I said. "I've always enjoyed having you in my class. I thought you enjoyed my class. Am I mistaken?"

"No, Ms. B. I like your class."

"Do you think that I should accept Jesus as the messiah as your note said? I want you to be perfectly honest with me. Do you think that I should no longer practice Judaism?"

"No, Ms. B."

"I really want you to be honest, Greg. I want to know how you feel about me as a person. Do you think less of me because I practice a different religion? Do you dislike me because I'm not Catholic?"

"No, Ms. B."

"Well, honestly, I thought we had a good relationship and we accepted each other for who we are. I didn't think we saw each other only as a Jew and a Catholic. I thought we liked each other as individuals. I didn't think it mattered what religion we each practice."

"Yes, Ms. B."

"Greg, please don't just be polite. I want to know how you honestly feel."

"I'm telling you the truth, Ms. B."

"Okay, Greg. I believe you."

"What did you think of me when you met me at the beginning of the year? Did I seem any different to you because of my religion?"

"No, Ms. B. You act like a teacher."

"Do you feel any differently about me or about Jewish people in general after all this? What exactly do you think?"

"I just feel bad about the whole thing."

"Oh."

"Have you learned anything from this whole experience? Tell me honestly, please."

"Well, I shouldn't just go along with what somebody

else does."

"That's for sure! Do you know that throughout history Jews and people of other religions have been persecuted for their beliefs? Do you know what that means?"

"Yes, sort of."

"What does it mean?"

"That those people were treated badly because of it."

"Yes. Have you heard of Hitler? Do you know what he did?"

"Yes, I think so."

"Hitler believed in an Aryan race which means he believed that only Caucasians with blonde or light hair should exist. He felt that only white, Christian people deserved to live. He murdered six million Jews in concentration camps and gas chambers because he felt they didn't belong on this planet. Six million people, Greg. He exterminated all of them just because of their religion. Do you understand what that means?

"He killed a lot of people."

"Yes. Is it right to kill people if they are different from us?"

"No."

"Is it right to treat them differently?"

"No."

"Have you heard of the KKK — the Ku Klux Klan?"

"I think so."

"Do you know what they did and what they do, because they still exist today?"

"They killed people too?"

"Yes, they hate Jews also. Not only that, they would kill

African Americans because they believe that people with dark or black skin shouldn't exist. They believe that they are an inferior race. What do you think of that?"

"I think that's wrong."

I need to teach him about other prejudices and discrimination too.

"In the 1920s klansmen, wearing white robes and masks, would lynch African Americans. Do you know what lynching is?"

"No, Ms. B."

"They would put ropes around their necks and hang them from trees."

"Uggh."

"Yeah, uggh. Pretty nasty, huh?"

"Yeah."

"What gives one person the right to judge someone else? If there's one thing I want you to take away with you today, it's that we have to be accepting of everyone. And in addition, I totally agree with you. You need to think for yourself and not be swayed by other people. If you allow that to happen, you could end up in a worse situation and people could get hurt. I sincerely hope that you learned that as our constitution says, everyone is equal and has rights. And we need to let people live their lives the way they want to and not the way we think they should unless they are hurting others. Do you understand?"

"Yes, Ms. B."

"Greg, do you really understand what I'm saying?"

"Yes, Ms. B."

"Can you say something so that I know you understand?"

"Yes, Ms. B. We shouldn't judge other people by their

religions or their beliefs. We should accept everyone for the way they are."

"Greg, I don't want you to just repeat what I say and act like you go along with me. I want to know what you honestly think."

"I agree with you, Ms. B. People shouldn't be treated differently just because they might be different from others."

"Okay, Greg. You'll be moving on to high school next year, and I hope you take this lesson with you. I hope you take this with you for the rest of your life actually. It's one of the most important things we could discuss."

"Yes, Ms. B."

"Thank you for coming to talk to me during your religion class. Was there anything else you want to say?"

"No, Ms. B."

"You may go back to your class."

"Thank you, Ms. B."

He left the room.

I had ranted. I sounded preachy. I couldn't help myself. I hope I said the right things. I hope I didn't forget anything important. I hope I got through to him. I hope I made a difference. I hope he was being truthful with me. This wasn't what I expected to be teaching this year, but it certainly was as important as teaching English Language Arts. I hope he turns out to be a better person because of this whole incident. I hope he's on the right path for his future. I certainly hope he has become more open-minded, and that he will grow up to be a really great person and contribute great things to our world. I know he has it in him. Children are our hope for the future.

Chapter 15

Amen

As much as word had spread about my discovery of the perpetrator, nobody mentioned it after Greg and I had our conversation. I heard nothing from any parents or school staff. The teachers didn't mention it, except for the religion teacher who ducked into my room again to ask me, "How did your conversation with Greg go?"

"Fine," I answered.

"Did you say everything you wanted to say? Do you think it made a difference?"

"I certainly got everything off my chest. Hopefully it made an impression on him."

"Yes, we can only hope….So I understand Nicholas was a part of this as well?"

"Yes, Greg told me that also."

How does she know this too? She must have talked with Mrs. A. Why do I continue to keep Mrs. A as my confidant?

"You probably want to speak with Nicholas as well, don't you?"

"Well, that would be a good idea."

"Unfortunately he's in math class during your planning period, and you are teaching when he is in my religion class."

Does she have everyone's schedule memorized, or did she look his up for me?

"Maybe I could take him out of math class or see him before or after school or during lunch."

"Maybe, but I don't think that will be easy for you to arrange. Would you like for me to talk to him? It's no problem really."

"Are you sure?"

"Oh, yes. I might even enjoy having such a conversation with him."

"Well, if you wouldn't mind, that'll be fine."

"Okay. I'll let you know what he says."

Once again she ambled down the hall.

A conversation with Nicholas is one less thing for me to worry about, I suppose. I don't know him very well, but she does. I'm sure she'll know what to say. Maybe she'll set him straight better than I could. We'll see what comes of this. I hope I didn't make a mistake. Maybe I should have arranged to talk to him myself. I'm sure it'll be fine whatever she does.

***

It was the last week of school and time for eighth grade graduation. It was scheduled during the school day so the whole school could attend. Parents and relatives were invited. As always, I had no idea what to expect or even

191

where the ceremony would be held. Of course it was in the big church.

I took my sixth grade homeroom to the service and sat with them as usual. I looked around at all the eighth grade graduates. Greg was chatting with Ryan next to him.

I wonder how many kids know what Greg and Nicholas did. In this school it seems as if everybody knows about everything. Greg doesn't appear to be bothered by any of it, which is good. I hope though that he is different inside.

I glanced over at Nicholas. The religion teacher, Mrs. H, had popped her head into my room again a few days after our last conversation.

"I did speak to Nicholas," she said. "He didn't have much to say except that he was sorry. I told him he should apologize to you himself."

"Oh, okay. That was it? He didn't say anything else at all?"

"Nope. I only had a few minutes to spend with him. He did seem sincere though."

"Oh, okay. Thanks."

I could have done better myself. Only a few minutes to cover something as important as this? I wonder what exactly she said to him. It doesn't really matter. Maybe I'll have a chance to say something to him when he comes to me to apologize.

The graduation ceremony was another regular church service except for the part where each student was called to receive a diploma. I was thankful that I didn't have to go up on the altar or say anything. At one point in the service, the teachers were asked to stand and be recognized. That I could handle. All the students received a blessing, and the service was over within an hour. The eighth graders returned to their classes for the remainder of the day. *That was a disappointment. What was so great about that? I expected something more ceremonial. They didn't even play the graduation march.*

***

I wanted to do something special for my eighth graders, so I did what I like to do—I wrote. I wrote them a piece I titled "Tribute to an Eighth Grade English Class," and I read it to them on one of our last days together.

It started:

I will always remember my eighth grade class my first year of teaching at this school. It was difficult enough coming into a new school, but then I was told to beware of my eighth grade class.

The first few days I didn't think there was anything of which I needed to be aware. I couldn't get these children to open their mouths and speak. I was worried they were too introverted and they would sit there like "bumps on a log" the entire school year. I soon discovered that I had totally misjudged the entire situation.

I went on to describe each student and tell what was special about each one. I looked at each student as I read, and they were all smiles. We laughed together at some of the details I included about each of their personalities. I ended the tribute with:

My heart goes out to each and every one of these students. I hope they realize how much they are truly loved and the potential they each have within themselves to make all their dreams come true. Every one of these children is special, and I know in my heart that they have brilliant futures ahead of them. G-d look after them and bless them all. I will truly miss them.

I must have been influenced by all those church services to write the part about the Lord looking out for them! I gave each student a copy of my tribute. They seemed to appreciate the piece. I meant every word of it. I don't know if they understood that when I wrote they are truly loved, I meant not only by their families and friends, but also by me. I loved them as if they were my own children. It was probably better that I did not have my own children at the time so that I could focus on these kids and the work involved with teaching them. I was able to dedicate a lot of time and effort and give these children what they needed to grow. In the early 1900s, teachers were required to be single for this very reason.

I have run into a few of my former students in my everyday travels, and they still remember me. I know it's a former student when I am addressed as "Ms. B." I can barely recognize them.

One time at a local fruit stand, the lady behind the counter tilted her head and examined me closely.

"Ms. B?"

"Yes?"

"It's me...Margaret Mulcahy.

Another time I ran into a former student working in the local shoe store. She helped me find a pair of sneakers. Another time, a former student worked at my automotive repair shop. He was happy to offer me a complimentary car wash. I didn't realize the job had perks years later!

They've turned into fine individuals whom I'm proud to say I taught and that have taught me as well. Of course seeing them reminds me of the tribulations I had at that school, but it was worth all the aggravation.

***

It was the last middle school teacher meeting of the year. I was sitting in the science lab, and we were discussing what we needed to do to close up our classrooms and end the school year. The science teacher put a contract for next year in front of each of us. The other teachers were obviously prepared for this. Right away they signed and handed the paper back. Nobody had prepared me. I had given little thought to next year, as I just wanted to make it to the end of this one. I hadn't applied for any other teaching positions. I hadn't the time to even look into it. I had nowhere else to go. Nobody made a big deal of the contract or asked me if I was going to sign. It seemed to be expected.

I read it over as quickly as I could without drawing attention to myself. Of course I was the only one reading it. I picked up my pen, signed on the dotted line, and held it up to be collected as the science teacher was taking the last ones.

Whew! That was close. I don't think anyone noticed my surprise or my conflict about the contract. Wasn't there a better way to handle this? Shouldn't this have been done on a private, individual basis? Did I just get railroaded? Did I really just sign on for the next school year after all that I went through this year? I suppose I can get out of my contract if I find another school. I better get on that.

I noticed on the contract that if I backed out after a certain date, I owed the school $500. Five hundred dollars?! They barely paid us anything, but I would owe them all that money!! The date was about a month away. There wasn't much time if I wanted to find another job.

Did I really just sign on again to deal with all this aggravation and ill treatment for another year? Have I lost my mind? Did I just give into peer pressure? Would that even be considered peer pressure since nobody said anything to me? Why didn't I say I needed time to think about it? Surely they all must know how hard this school year has been for me. Why did they handle it in that manner? I guess in this instance I got treated like every other teacher. But I'm not like everyone else. Well, maybe I'll find another job. Let's hope.

I was already enrolled in an intensive six-credit eight-week summer institute for teachers at a local university. The program, called the Maryland Writing Project Summer Institute, consisted of teachers instructing other teachers how to improve the teaching of writing, and class started right away. This class was going to take up the majority of my summer. I still had to buy books and supplies. I skimmed help wanted ads in the newspaper, but other than that, I didn't really have time to do a full-out job search. I didn't see any other teaching positions that would interest me. I tried contacting the county again, but they still had no

196

apparent interest in hiring me. And at that time, they had very few, if any, openings for English teachers.

So I never backed out of my contract. Come September I was back in my same classroom for year two in the Catholic school.

Oh my gosh! Am I insane? Have I completely lost my mind?! I guess I'm just a glutton for punishment!! I'm doing this again! Well at least this year there should be fewer surprises, and I'll know what to expect. Here I am again working like a dog for such little pay and no appreciation. Hopefully this school year will be different. Hopefully the school year won't start with another nasty note on my desk. Nicholas never apologized to me in person. I hope he was truly sorry for what he did. Hopefully, by now, everyone has accepted the idea of a Jew teaching in a Catholic school.

Chapter 16

Hear, O Israel

My second school year started much smoother. I understood what they were talking about during the meetings before school started. The church service for the faculty wasn't as traumatic for me. And this time we didn't have to go up on the altar and hold hands. Why couldn't they have skipped it the first year?

My seventh and eighth graders were already familiar since they were my sixth and seventh graders the previous year. I had to learn only the names of the sixth graders. The fifth grade teachers, Mrs. E and Mrs. F, continued to be very nice and told me to ask them if I had any questions. I had Mrs. E's daughter in my sixth grade class last year, so this year she was in seventh. Kathleen was a pleasure. Mrs. F would chat with me in the hallway sometimes when we were standing there for hall duty. Her two daughters were in the lower school.

I started the school year with the same unit as the previous year. While I reviewed my lesson plans from last year, I never reused them. I would rewrite them, since I would come up with new teaching ideas and the students were different. I didn't feel as much hostility from the parents and staff as I did last year. I knew they still were unhappy that I was there, but I suppose they accepted that I wasn't going anywhere.

The school year was going along fine until I had a medical issue. On a Saturday morning in the beginning of October I woke up around one a.m. in pain. I had a terrible ache on the side of my abdomen.

Oh, it's probably gas. It should go away. I'll try to go back to sleep.

I lay awake for hours.

It doesn't feel like my stomach. What is this?

I tried using a heating pad. It still hurt.

I took some Tylenol, and the pain subsided for a couple of hours.

I fell back to sleep. When the Tylenol wore off, I woke up in pain again.

I rolled over to my other side. That position briefly alleviated the pain, and I dozed for a short while.

Around seven a.m. the pain increased, so I called my parents. My mother told me to call the doctor's office and call her back. Within a half hour, the doctor returned my call and told me to come into the office. My mother picked me up and drove me. After an examination, the general physician didn't know what was wrong with me. He recommended I go see my gynecologist, and his office called and made an appointment for me immediately.

Gynecologist? Why do I need to see her? I don't think the doctor knows what he's talking about.

My mother drove me to the gynecologist. The office was only ten minutes away, but it seemed like an hour, because, by this time, my side felt as though someone was taking a hammer to it from the inside. To make matters worse, my mother sat at a red light when I begged her to go through it. There were no cars in front of us and no oncoming traffic.

"Diane, I have to obey the traffic rules," she explained, as I was moaning and holding my side.

Obeying traffic rules is more important than your daughter's health? Really, mom? If I was bleeding, would you still be sitting at the light? Why do you think ambulances are allowed to pass other vehicles? Because it's an emergency!

It seemed to be another five minutes before the light turned green.

Again, the doctor didn't know what was wrong with me.

"I'm sending you for an x-ray," my gynecologist said.

"An x-ray?"

"Yes. We need to see what's going on in there. You can go straight there from here."

My mother drove me to the radiologist. Fortunately, that wasn't far either, and we didn't hit any red lights.

After my x-ray, they told me to go back to the dressing room to change out of the hospital gown. I changed, barely able to turn around in this space the size of a gym locker. I opened the curtain and stood there for several minutes. Doctors, nurses, and lab technicians scuffled past me. I stopped someone who said somebody would be right with me. Nobody came. I didn't know where I should go, so I sat down on the bench inside this closet. My pain had temporarily abated, and I sat waiting and watching. I over-heard two technologists several feet away.

"That's strange. We can't see her ovaries in this picture."

"Yes, that is strange. I wonder why."

What? Are they talking about another patient? No, I know they're talking about me. For one thing, they took a picture of my reproductive system. How many other people have they x-rayed in the last few minutes in that area of their body? I know they're talking about me, because that's the way my luck runs.

Why can't they see my ovaries? Oh my gosh! What's wrong with me? This sounds serious! I need to breathe and not hyperventilate. Deep breaths—-in and out, in and out. Let's wait and see what they tell me.

By the time somebody came to get me, I was sitting on the bench with my knees up to my chest, my body shaking. I was in pain again and feeling such anxiety that I could barely stand up.

"We're sending you back to your gynecologist with the x-rays," the lady told me. "You will have to discuss this with her."

She extended the x-rays to me.

What? They don't know what's wrong with me either? If I hadn't overheard that conversation, I would have thought that they just wanted my gynecologist to give me the results. But I know the truth. And now there will be more waiting. That's what I need right now— to be bounced around like a rubber ball without anybody helping me when I'm in pain. How long will I have to endure this? Why can't somebody help me? How can these doctors not know what's wrong with me? Didn't they go to medical school?!

My mother and I waited only a few minutes before my gynecologist called us into her office.

"I'm admitting you to the hospital."

My mother gasped.

"What? Are you kidding? The hospital?" I asked.

"Yes," she said. "You need to go to the hospital."

"I really don't think that's necessary," I replied.

"Yes, it is. And I recommend you go now. You don't even need to go home and pack. Go right to the hospital. They are waiting for you. I already told them you are coming."

"Really? Are you sure?"

"Yes, I'm sure."

"Is this a life or death emergency?"

"No, but we need to figure out what's going on, and we shouldn't wait."

My mother drove. We walked right up to the front desk, and the receptionist said there was a room ready for me.

They didn't have to be so fast. I wouldn't mind waiting here. I really don't want to go.

She put an ID bracelet on my wrist. After filling out some forms, I was escorted to my room.

My gynecologist came to see me that evening. Both my parents were in the room.

"We are going to have to open you up to see what's going on," she said.

"What? Surgery???!!!"

"Yes, that's the only way we can figure out what's going on. We have to do exploratory surgery. I won't know anything until I can look around in there. We'll operate tomorrow."

"Tomorrow????!!!"

"Yes, tomorrow. I'll see you then."

They prepped me for surgery that night. The IV didn't bother me that much, nor did the catheter. What really upset me was the long tube the nurse was holding.

"What's that?" I asked.

"We have to empty out your stomach."

"What? Using that?"

"Yes."

"No," I said, shaking my head.

"Yes," she said, shaking her head affirmatively.

I might as well submit. This lady isn't going to back down.

First thing the next morning, they wheeled me into the operating room and told me to count backwards from 100. I made it to 97. I don't remember ever falling asleep so fast.

When I awoke, I was in a small holding area on a stretcher. A nurse was standing over me.

"I see that you're awake," she said. "Let me know when you're in pain, and I'll give you something for it." She walked away.

"Oh, okay.....Ouch!! Oh!!! Youch!! Now!!!" I yelled only seconds later, feeling a searing pain down my abdomen as if someone had cut me open and sewed me back together.

Fortunately, the nurse was only a few steps away. She must have had the needle in her hand, because she injected it STAT into my IV, and the pain slowly subsided. I breathed a sigh of relief.

Good heavens, I hope I don't have to feel that pain again. I thought my body was going to self-destruct. Surely the nurse would have known that it was only a matter of moments before I needed medicine. She could have stood there and waited. Heck, she could have even held my hand.

"Read that clock on the wall and tell me what time it is," she said, pointing to a clock high up on the wall a few yards to my right.

"I'm not wearing my glasses. I can't see it."

Read the clock on the wall? Why? Does she want to see if I'm lucid? Does she think the pain took me to a crazy place?

She put my glasses on my face, and I read that it was shortly after 11:30 am.

"Okay," she said and left to care for another patient.

Is it that late already? How many hours have I been in surgery? What did they do to me? Did they find anything? Did they take out any of my internal organs? At least I'm still alive. At least I woke up. This nurse obviously isn't talking, and I'm too weak to shout out to find someone to answer all these questions. I guess I'll just wait.

"You won't be in recovery much longer," she told me about a half hour later.

Oh, I'm in the recovery room. I won't be here much longer? It feels like I've already been here for hours.

I looked at the clock since I could see it now. Only a half hour had passed.

What are they going to do with me now? I hope they don't discharge me after they just opened me up! What did they do to me? I guess the doctor will come in and tell me she didn't find anything, and I'm okay.

The doctor didn't come in. They wheeled me out of recovery, and my parents came right over to me.

"Everything's okay, Diane," my mother said, taking my hand.

"Yes," I answered groggily, looking through the slits in my eyes.

Yes, everything is okay; I'm alive.

I closed my eyes again. I just wanted to rest.

"They found ovarian cysts," my mother informed me in her usual loudspeaker-like voice that could broadcast over a football stadium. "That means cysts on your ovaries. It was nothing serious. They removed them. They left most of your ovaries."

"Oh, okay.....Mom?"

"Yes?"

"Where are we?"

"We're out in the hallway."

"Can we discuss this in private? Maybe in my room? Do we need to discuss this in front of everyone?"

That's my mother—always blasting my business all over the place for everyone to hear. I don't think my dad even wants to be a part of this discussion! He looks embarrassed.

"Oh, she's fine," my mother said to my father and the technician pushing my stretcher. "She hasn't changed a bit."

I was wheeled to my room, and my parents stayed until my father tired and said he wanted to go home.

***

My mother informed me she had called the school to tell them I was in the hospital, and I wouldn't be there on Monday. She told them she didn't know when I'd be back.

205

Knowing my mother, she probably told them exactly why I was in the hospital and the whole faculty would know.

This is embarrassing. I don't want the entire faculty to know that I had a problem with my reproductive system. It would be different if I could say I had a hernia or even a fracture of some sort. But my ovaries feel really personal!

After about a week in the hospital, I was discharged, and my parents took me to their house to convalesce. I stayed in my former bedroom. I couldn't walk the two flights up to my apartment, and the doctor told me I couldn't do any heavy lifting and to take it easy for a couple of months.

The principal called a day or two later, and my mother handed me the phone.

"How are you?" he asked.

I'd feel better talking to you if you were a woman. At least you'd be able to relate.

"Feeling a little better every day," I said.

"Good. So when did the doctor say you could come back to work?"

Oh, right. Let's get to business. I forgot this wouldn't be purely a social call.

"Well, you might want to be sitting down for this one."

"I'm fine," he said.

"Ten weeks. The doctor said I shouldn't return to work for ten weeks!"

Ten weeks!! What a long time!! That's such a long time to leave my students. That's over two months!! What are they going to do without me?

"Okay," Mr. Z said, sounding calm and unconcerned.

Does he even care that my students will be without me for over two months? Doesn't he realize how bad this is? Maybe he's happy to replace me for a while.

"We'll get a long-term substitute," he said.

"Oh, okay."

The school has long-term subs? Where do you find those?

"We'll need you to send in lessons plans until we get a long-term substitute."

"Oh, okay," I replied.

What? I still have to work in this condition? Will I still get a paycheck for this? I just had surgery, and I'm expected to write lesson plans? Why can't I say no to people?

"I'll have the sub call you every day, and you can read the plan to her over the phone."

"Oh, okay."

"We'll see you in December."

"Yes, thanks."

He hung up.

A long-term sub? And I have to tell the daily subs what to do? My parents are going to have to go to my apartment and get my teaching supplies. Boy, the work never stops even when you are laid up. So much for resting. And who are they going to get to temporarily replace me?

***

A week or so later I was on the phone with a substitute teacher I didn't know, explaining what she should be doing with the children that day. By this point, I was sore, but I was able to walk around. It was as if I'd had a C-section but not delivered a baby! As the days went by, I kept wondering how many different substitutes my students would have and how long it would take to find a long-term substitute.

About a week after that, I got a phone call from Mrs. A. She wanted to know all about my surgery.

Wow. I'm surprised she hasn't called me sooner. She always wants all the gossip.

"What does the incision look like? Where did they cut you?" she asked." I want to see it. You'll have to show it to me when I see you."

Great, I can't wait to show you my patchwork in a relatively private part of my body.

"What unit have you been working on with the kids?" she asked me.

Don't you know? Didn't you talk to the substitute? Where did the plans that I dictated over the phone end up? In the trash can?

She said they had a long-term substitute who would fully take over, and I didn't have to make any more lesson plans.

Thank goodness. Maybe now I can actually focus on recuperating.

She called back a week later.

"Diane, the long-term substitute has all the journals from all the kids in each class, and she was wondering if someone could drop them by and you could look them over."

"What? Read their journals?"

"Yes. She'd really appreciate it."

"Oh, uh...okay," I stammered.

Isn't it part of the substitute's job to do the grading? Why did I say yes again?

Not long after, a parent volunteer I didn't recognize was knocking at our door. She thrust a crate of journals at me.

I took them from her and, after realizing how heavy they were, put them down immediately.

Crap. I shouldn't have picked that up. The doctor said no heavy lifting.

When I looked up again, the figure was fleeing toward the car.

That was a fast getaway. Afraid I might change my mind? Or perhaps she's just the delivery person. Or maybe she wants nothing to do with me but had to deliver the goods.

I shut the door.

Why did I agree to do this? I wonder if the long-term substitute is incapable. Or are they just taking advantage of me? Oh well. At least I get to be a little involved. Plus I get to communicate with my students. At least they'll know I'm still around, and I will be coming back. Let's see what they're working on and what they wrote. Journal writing is always interesting.

I spent several days reading the journal entries. There wasn't much. The first batch was only from the sixth grade class, and each student had only written one paragraph or less about a short story they read.

What assignment did they get? Wouldn't you think if I had to read these over, someone would tell me what the writing assignment was? They'd never get away with this if I were there. They'd be writing so much more and adding a lot more detail to their writing.

Not one student wrote me a note! There's nothing personal in here at all. Didn't the kids know I'd be reading these? Maybe nobody told them. How disappointing. Not even a hello.

I simply responded to each student's writing. I think a couple of journals were missing, because I didn't see one from every student.

A few days later I got a second delivery of journals from my seventh grade class, and the sixth grade journals were picked up.

I'm so disappointed. I wonder if the substitute was watching closely over them and instructed them not to write anything personal. Just a little note saying hello or that I am missed or asking how I'm doing would have been nice. And I still have no idea what she is teaching them. This work doesn't look like it's related to any of the lessons or the unit that I had provided. She certainly isn't using the journals the way they were intended. I can't wait to go back to school and get these students back on track. I hope the kids will be happy to see me.

I read and responded to the seventh grade journals, and then it was another pick-up and delivery of the eighth grade journals.

When I reached for the journals at the bottom of the crate, I found Get Well cards and notes!!

Hallelujah! I'm not forgotten after all!

Emily drew me an adorable picture of three Dalmatians labeled with the girls' names. Ryan cut and paste a face out of construction paper. My eighth grade class all signed one large card. Another card was from all the kids in one family, which was especially thoughtful because I didn't teach them all. I also received a banner with drawings and a few signatures but mostly a lot of blank space. Did students forget to sign, I wondered.

The shocker was the homemade card I got from four lower school teachers. The outside said, "To Diane: Get well soon. We miss you."

The inside read:

Dear Diane:

We were so sorry to hear about your "condition." It's happened to people in my family, so I know how painful and inconvenient it is. The most important thing is that you are OK and on the road to recovery. The kiddos miss you and so do the teachers. Do what the doctor says and hurry back! See you soon.

Love,

They listed their names.

The first name was the teacher/parent who yelled at me last year about my eighth grade class.

Wow. Are they serious? I didn't think these teachers even liked me. This card was so thoughtful. It seems to be written with such feeling. They miss me?! What do I make of this? These teachers have barely spoken to me, and I don't work closely with them. And, as I suspected, the entire faculty knows my "condition." I hope this is sincere, but it's hard for me to believe.

Mrs. A called again.

"Nobody can pick up the journals. Can you bring them to school tomorrow?"

"Well....I guess so....but my mother will have to drive me. I'm not allowed to drive yet."

"Okay. I'll meet you behind the school by the church at noon during lunch."

"Okay," I agreed.

My mother drove me, and Mrs. A was standing there waiting. I handed her the crate since I was able to lift it by this time.

"Let me see," Mrs. A said, putting the crate down.

"What?"

"Let's see the scar."

"Oh. It's still so fresh. I don't think you want to see it."

"Yes, I do. Let's see."

"Well, I'd have to push my pants down a little bit. I'm not sure you want to see that far down!"

"Push them down. I'm not going to see anything I haven't seen before. Let me take a peek."

I pushed my pants down slightly and opened my waistband wide so she could see my scar.

"Oh, wow. That's a nice scar. I have to get back. Let us know what your exact date of return will be when you know it. See you then!"

Did she not believe me, and she had to see the proof herself? Does she think I made this all up—that I needed to take a break from teaching for a couple of months?

My mother didn't say much on the ride back. She had stayed in the car, and I didn't even think to introduce her to Mrs. A., and Mrs. A hadn't asked to meet her either.

Why did I do that? Why did I show Mrs. A my scar? She didn't need to see that. I shouldn't have listened to her. I feel like she just invaded my privacy. Was that really necessary? Why do I always give in to people? I have to stop being so nice.

***

I returned to my apartment after six weeks. I was happy to be home. My friend, Adeline, came to visit, and we decided to color my hair. I was nervous because I've never changed my hair color. She put the dye in my hair, and it splattered all over the bathroom, leaving a permanent stain on the wall. My hair ended up a darker shade of brown even though I was trying to lighten it.

In addition to that, I decided since I wasn't doing much of anything, now was the time to switch to contact lenses. I had always wanted them, and I was pretty sick of wearing glasses. So when I was allowed to resume driving, I went to the ophthalmologist. They gave me a practice set, and I was thrilled that I was able to get them in and out of my eyes, even if it took me about forty minutes.

When my prescription contact lenses came in, I picked them up from the store and tried to insert them and remove them myself at home. It took me a half hour to get them in and another half hour to get them out of my eyes.

Boy, I'm going to have to get up at five a.m. to wear my contact lenses if I don't start getting faster.

But by the time I was scheduled to return to school, I was almost a pro.

***

When I returned to school mid-December, it was a few weeks before Christmas break which worked out well, because I could work those weeks and then get more rest over vacation. I still didn't have all my energy back. As a matter of fact, I couldn't stand for long periods of time. During that first week back, I had to sit down wherever and whenever I could, which was usually resting my rear end on a vacant desk or the back ledge. I was accustomed to standing most of the day, walking around my classroom and the building, so I found it frustrating.

In the faculty room my first morning back, a few

teachers commented on my appearance.

"Oh my gosh. You're thin as a rail."

"Wow, you lost a lot of weight. And you couldn't stand to lose that much in the first place."

How about a "Welcome back" or even "You look good, considering"? It would be nice if somebody said that they were happy to see me. I suppose a hug was out of the question.

When I made it down to my classroom, my homeroom children were already there preparing for the day. None of them even looked up at me.

Wow. Isn't anybody around here happy to see me? Can't they even act like I was gone a while?

"Hello everyone," I said. "It's good to see you all again."

I heard some murmurs. Nobody addressed me.

Maybe they're annoyed that I was gone so long. Or maybe they're put off my different appearance. Well, I don't know these kids as well as the other grades. Maybe they really liked the substitute.

It was the same story in first period.

Isn't anybody happy to see me? I'm so happy to see them. Maybe they aren't happy because they know that they will be getting some real work now. It's not my fault that I had to leave them. I couldn't help it. I didn't want to leave. I'm so happy to be back.

I taught the lesson I had planned which was to start fresh with a brand new unit. I thought it would be fun to do poetry. I never received any plans from the long-term substitute briefing me on what was taught or how the students were doing.

Wouldn't you think I'd receive something filling me in? What's that all about? Oh well. I'll ask the kids what they did and then start over on my own.

I went home that first night and looked in mirror. I was

wearing a purple outfit, one of my favorites, a shirt with embroidered flowers on it and a matching skirt. I looked closer at my reflection.

Wow. They are right. I really did lose a lot of weight. I'm actually too skinny! My full skirt isn't full at all; it's hanging limp over my hips and thighs and swinging back and forth like a gorilla's arms when I walk. If I lose any more weight, I'll look like a cadaver! My face looks drawn as well. Plus, with my darkened hair and my contact lenses, maybe I frightened the students! Maybe they think I'm a "purple people eater," an alien who swings from trees in a 1958 song of the same name by Sheb Wooley. I'll have to gain my weight back and start looking recognizable again.

After only a few days, the students seemed to adjust to having me back. Whatever unfriendliness or distance I felt had dissipated. We were all engrossed in reading and writing limericks, couplets, cinquains and sonnets. We wrote epigrams, epitaphs, odes and elegies. It didn't take me long to get my weight back up to 110 pounds instead of the 90 pounds from my infirmity. I picked up a lot of carry-out on my way home. I indulged in a lot of double-scooped hot fudge sundaes. My hair had grown out so that my face brightened with my natural color. Except for the contact lenses (that nobody commented on except Mrs. A to ask how long it takes to put them in), I was looking and acting like my old self by the time we returned from Christmas break.

Chapter 17

the Lord our G-d

A few weeks after we returned from winter vacation, I was conducting a writing workshop with my seventh graders. I'd often share my writing with them, just as they would share theirs with classmates and me. I decided I wanted to share what I had written about my time in the hospital.

I pulled up a chair to the front of the room. They were "all ears."

"I titled this piece 'My Ten Day Vacation,'" I told them. Anna raised her hand.

"Yes?"

"Ms. B, is this about your trip to the hospital?"

"Why yes, it is. How did you know that?"

"Just a guess." Others were nodding their head as if they too had already known.

"Raise your hand if you already figured that out."

Ninety percent of the kids raised their hands.

"Well there goes that surprise," I said. I started to read:

> As I stepped up to the long, marble topped
> counter, I said to the clerk, "I'd like one room,

please."

She replied, "You must be Diane."

"Yes," I answered. "How did you know?"

"We've been expecting you. Please complete these forms," she said as she pushed them in my direction. "You may sit over there if you need to sit down."

"No, thank you," I said. "I'll be fine right here at the counter."

After I completed the forms and slid them back over the counter, the clerk extracted more information from me, including my address and telephone number, typing the information into some machine behind the counter as we spoke. She put a bracelet around my wrist (a welcome present I thought) and said, "This gentleman will show you to your room."

He carried my bag, and I followed him down a long corridor, up four flights in the elevator, and halfway around the building before he swung open a door and announced, "This is your room."

I stepped into a room that was the size of my kitchen. The bed was pushed up against the sink, the curtain was hanging off the rod, and the room was so small that one could literally roll off the bed and land in the bathroom.

"This is it?" I asked in total disbelief. *This is all I get for the enormous amount of money they probably charge?*

"Yes, this is it," he responded. "It is rather small, but comfortable. The nurse will be in to speak with you in a minute," he said as he left my cubicle. So began my ten day "vacation" at Northwest Medical Center.

Peter's sister, Brianna, raised her hand.

"Yes, Brianna?"

"Can you still have children?"

"What?"

"Are you able to have children?"

"What makes you ask me that?" I could barely breathe. I was in shock over the question.

"The substitute told us you had a problem with your ovaries. Can you still have children?"

"She told you that?"

"Yes." All the children were nodding their heads.

"You all knew what happened to me?"

Again, they were all nodding.

For these kids to even know that problems with your ovaries have to do with bearing children, they must have had an in-depth discussion. Oh my goodness!

I was having a hot flash unrelated to my reproductive system. My whole body was burning. I grew so angry that if the kids weren't there, I would have gone outside to scream. I literally wanted to scream—one of those screams that is so

218

loud it would have shattered the windows. My room would have been nice and airy after that and maybe I would have felt liberated. I knew the feeling that came over my body was what they mean by the expression "make my blood boil." My blood was a boilin'!

How dare the substitute. How dare all of them. Why should these kids know my personal business? If I had been the substitute, I would have said something about how the teacher was in the hospital, but she's going to be okay and returning soon. I would have told them that any further questions should be directed to the teacher when she returns or even to the principal.

I had to suppress my anger, as I had to finish class. Plus, I couldn't take my anger out on the kids. They were just innocent victims of the unethical, ignorant school staff. So I took a deep breath and tapped into my inner Zen.

"Yes, I can still have children," I answered. "I'm fine."

I'll have to deal with this fiasco later.

I continued to read my story to them:

> I watched the leaves change colors from my bolted shut, never-to-be-opened window and listened to exclamations of "Oh, isn't it a beautiful autumn day" and "Everyone should go outdoors today" from passersby and television forecasters. I came to the realization that there will be no sightseeing on this trip.
>
> But, none the less, room service was outstanding. Although food was not delivered for five days, I had other forms of service instead.
>
> Never once did the phlebotomists fail to draw

219

my blood every day. One morning I told the lady that my only request was that she warn me before she sticks me. After she stabbed the needle into my arm, she squeaked, "Prick. . . There. Did you hear me say it?" I only wished I had a needle meant for her in my hand.

And then there was the evening I was told I would be receiving the service that would clean my body out altogether. I opened my hospital door to find the nurse holding a very long plastic tube. "Excuse me, but could we have a chat about that tube?" I whined. She never replied verbally, but proceeded to fully service my transmission that night.

I was even required to sign permission slips for the two field trips I took out of my room while never leaving the resort itself.

The first trip took me downstairs to the CAT scan room where three hours and six bad-tasting glasses of something beforehand had prepared me for this excursion. The release form I signed mentioned something about the risk of heart failure, also known as death. The CAT scan machine whizzed and hummed as I held my breath. I couldn't remember signing any release forms for any amusement park rides I'd taken.

My second field trip, which also required a permission slip, was into the operating room. As they wheeled me down the hallway and I had braced myself for a long ride in this mammoth building, I asked, "So where exactly is the operating room?" Fifteen seconds after I asked, we pulled up in front of another set of double doors, and they told me I was there. "Gee, I was hoping for a long, slow ride. I'm not in any hurry," I whined as they pushed me through the doors.

Never travel without first consulting your map.

Over the remaining days, a parade of people came through my room: doctors, resident doctors, nurses, nurses' assistants, lab technicians, phlebotomists, cafeteria staff, hospital volunteers, maintenance workers, housekeepers, family members, friends, and concerned individuals.

One morning when the nurse awakened me at 4 A.M. to check my blood pressure and temperature, I moaned, "Does anyone ever get any rest in here?"

"No," she replied. "Never expect to get any rest in the hospital."

The following day when the hammering from the construction work beneath me ceased to desist and visitors were constantly streaming in and out, I asked another nurse, "Does anyone ever get any rest in the hospital?"

"Of course not," was her reply.

When my doctor came to visit, I asked her the same question and got the same answer, only her answer was accompanied by a laugh.

So much for any rest during this vacation.

The day I left, my father ran a card through the magnetic card reader, and the double doors to my ward swung open. "Freedom at last," I thought as tears streamed down my cheeks. He wheeled me out in a wheelchair while I was carrying my balloon and teddy bear, looking like a little girl who had been to a carnival. The wheelchair wheels churned as we made our way halfway around the building, down four flights in the elevator, and down a long corridor. As I exited the building, the "bellhop" from my first day whizzed by.

"Good-bye," I shouted.

"How are you?" he yelled from a distance.

"Leaving!" I answered.

"Late for a meeting," he replied.

And with that, I departed. I stood up from the wheelchair and stepped into my parents' limousine (their Honda Accord) to begin my ten day layover at the house of .... MY PARENTS!!!!

The children applauded when I finished. They had nothing but positive comments.

"I really enjoyed that, Ms. B."

"I liked how you compared your experience to a vacation."

I always asked for honest criticism, and I asked them how I could improve the piece.

"I think you should have been more specific," John commented.

"How?"

"You don't tell the reader what you were in the hospital for. The reader doesn't know why you were wheeled into the operating room."

No, the reader might not, but you all certainly do. I knew the question would come up eventually, and I was prepared to answer it after I read this piece aloud. I was going to tell you that I had a non-life-threatening growth removed in my abdomen, but I'm fine. Obviously it isn't necessary for me to share that with you now because of the stupidity of the faculty and staff who told you all of my business without consulting me first. I don't know how to deal with this.

I brought this up to Mrs. A.

"Did you know that all my students know why I was in the hospital?"

"What do you mean?"

"They all knew I had problems with my ovaries."

"How did they know that?"

Is she pretending to be ignorant and innocent? I wonder if she had a hand in this. I bet at least one of these teachers blabbed the specifics of my hospital visit to all the students in their classes. Either that or the students overheard them talking about it in the hallways. Maybe they announced it over the intercom. "We want to let everyone know that Ms. B is in the hospital. They operated on her and found that she had a problem with her ovaries. We'll keep you posted about whether or not she can have children."

"I was hoping *you* could tell *me*." I said to her.

"I guess the substitute told them."

"Did anyone else say anything to them?"

"I wouldn't know."

I don't remember telling the substitute about my condition. Someone else must have told her, and I don't appreciate that. There's nothing I can do about it now.

Thankfully, the interest in my reproductive system was short-lived, and I didn't have to field any more questions about it. I didn't have long to think about it anyway, as the next problem walked through my door shortly after.

Chapter 18

the Lord is One

It was almost Spring, and I was straightening up my classroom one day during my planning period, getting ready for my afternoon of eighth graders when Mr. Z came strutting in holding a bunch of papers.

"Ms. B, what have you been teaching for your grammar lessons?" he demanded.

"What?"

"What grammar have you been teaching the children?"

"Well, the students learn mostly independently and study different grammar principles according to what they need. I discuss it with each student, but they usually know what they are weak in."

Boy, I don't even get a hello. What did I do wrong now?

"Well it sounds like you aren't teaching them any grammar at all. Have you done one grammar lesson?"

"Sometimes I do a mini-lesson with the whole class on one thing, but we've been focused more on literature the last couple of weeks."

I see that the individual attention I'm giving each student is still unappreciated. Nobody around here seems to understand that it is unusual for students to actually work on their own level. In most instances, this is called tutoring, and parents pay dearly for it. Once again, my teaching practices are being criticized. I wonder which parents complained this time. Maybe they could teach this class instead.

"Well, from now on you will do a grammar lesson with each class every single day. Use these grammar worksheets."

He held them out, and I took them.

"Uh...okay..." I stammered.

"Do you understand? One worksheet each day."

"Okay."

He left the room before I could tell him how wrong this was. Okay, even if I had a chance, I wouldn't have been brave enough to stand up to him. He wouldn't have changed his mind anyway. I stood there holding these despicable grammar sheets that I knew the kids would find boring and monotonous.

Every day? I need to do this every day? Plus I will need to grade them or at least check them every day. Thanks so much for more boring work for me too.

I didn't have a choice, as I wanted to keep my job. So the next day I handed out the first set of grammar worksheets as the drill at the beginning of class.

"What's this, Ms. B?" I heard.

"What?? A grammar worksheet? Really?!" I heard coming from another direction.

"We don't have a choice," I explained.

"Why not? Nadine asked. "We're learning our grammar pretty well, I think."

Exactly. Even the kids know how ridiculous this is.

"Well, this is coming from the top that we have to complete this, so let's just get them done and move on."

Do they know what I mean by "coming from the top?" Are they going to argue with me?

The kids completed them, we reviewed the answers, and we put them away until we had a new sheet the next day. Thankfully they did not argue with me or ask what "coming from the top" meant. The kids didn't complain, even though it was obvious they found it demeaning. Sometimes we went over the answers together and sometimes I collected and checked them. Every now and then I'd assign them as homework so I could say the kids did it, and we didn't have to complete it in class.

Only a few more months, and we won't have to look at these stupid grammar worksheets anymore. Come on summer vacation!!

***

I was really looking forward to summer vacation, because this year I wanted to actually relax. I planned on spending time reading, swimming, and lounging by the pool reading. Last summer I attended the Maryland Writing Project Summer Institute. Although I gave up a large part of my summer break, it is where I became reinvigorated and where I learned a lot of innovative techniques I wasn't afraid to try in my classroom. I received six credits for taking the workshop which counted toward my accreditation, since I need six credits every five years to continue teaching. Anyone who thinks teachers are lucky to not work over the summer has no clue what they are talking about!

So I owe a big shout-out to the Maryland Writing Project who has inspired and motivated numerous teachers to be the best they can be. Their website www.towson.edu/mwp as of November 1, 2019 explains their mission and purpose:

> The Maryland Writing Project, housed in Towson University's College of Education since 1981, is a site of the National Writing Project. We are a teacher-driven professional development organization, where the area's best educators gather to research, teach and practice the most effective methods of teaching writing and using writing as a learning tool.
>
> The Maryland Writing Project believes that teachers are the best teachers of other teachers. Our mission is to identify, train and support excellent teachers so that they can share their knowledge and experience in writing instruction and writing to learn methods. These teacher-consultants research, develop and share best writing practices in order to effect change in their classrooms, schools, and school systems.

My time at the summer institute reading, writing, researching, preparing projects, sharing, learning and bonding widened my total vision and perspective. I learned not only how to improve my teaching of writing but my teaching of reading and other aspects of English Language Arts. I learned from experts in my own community as well as published experts, such as Lucy Calkins and Nancy Atwell, groundbreaking pioneers in the education field.

I attended Saturday workshops during the year and summer institute visitor days. As a Maryland Writing Project Teacher Consultant, I shared my knowledge with other teachers and garnered valuable information from them as well.

Unfortunately, I believe it was many of these techniques from the institute that irritated those traditionalists in this old-fashioned school. While I enjoyed trying new things with my students, it seemed to be too much for the adults. It all worked wonderfully with my students though!

Mrs. E told me her daughter, Kathleen, in my seventh grade class, had advanced more than one school year with her reading and writing. I knew that Kathleen wasn't the only student to show such progress. Mrs. E seemed impressed that Kathleen was doing so well, especially because writing had been a struggle for her in the past. She said that Kathleen enjoys it so much now that she was planning on attending the Maryland Writing Project Summer Student Institute this coming summer. This institute is where several Teacher Consultants conduct writing workshops for several weeks with the kids. I was thrilled to hear that Kathleen was enjoying writing so much that she was going to use part of her summer to do even more! The funny thing was that Mrs. E didn't know I am a Maryland Writing Project Teacher Consultant. They found this program on their own! I knew that while Kathleen may be the only student from this school attending the summer institute, my other students would use their new-found skills and enthusiasm for writing well into their future.

Chapter 19

G-d grant me the serenity to accept the things I cannot change

The secretary's voice crackled through the loud speaker in my classroom. "Ms. B, you have a telephone call. Please come to the office."

I had no idea who could be calling and why it would be so urgent that I was being hailed.

I hope something isn't wrong. Could it be my parents? Was there, heaven forbid, an accident? Did someone die?

It was afternoon at the latter end of my second year, and my eighth grade class was busily reviewing their speeches for the oratorical contest. This year my eighth grade class had double the amount of students. My afternoon was even more hectic than last year. The kids were working well, so I ducked into Mrs. A's room and told her that I was running to the office if she could listen for my students.

I trekked to the office where the school secretary directed me to take the call in a room across the lobby. I walked into a small room opposite the main office. It contained only one unattended desk with a phone. I had never been in this room before. As a matter of fact, I didn't even know this room existed! I picked up the phone and pressed the button for the line that was blinking.

"Hello?"

"Hello, Ms. B?"

"Yes."

"This is Mr. Williams from Baltimore City Public Schools."

"Yes?"

"This is Ms. B who applied for a teaching job in Baltimore City, correct?"

"Yes, it is."

Oh, is that who's calling? Oh crap. They called my school. I never told anyone here that I applied somewhere else. I really don't want them to know. I wonder if they told the school secretary who was calling. I wonder if anyone is listening on this line. Oh well. I can't hang up now.

"We're calling to let you know we have a position open in one of our middle schools next school year."

Hallelujah! Are they offering me a job? Sound calm.

"Oh, okay."

"Are you still available?"

"Yes, I am."

You betcha!

"Then we'll give your file to the principal, and you'll be hearing from him. Thank you very much."

"Okay. Thanks."

231

Mr. Williams hung up before I could find out which school it was!

I guess I'll just have to wait until I get another phone call. I hope they call me at home the next time.

Instead of immediately hanging up the phone, I listened for a second click to see if someone had been listening. I examined the phone and looked at the buttons. Other lines were in use, but I knew they couldn't connect. I could find no evidence of an eavesdropper.

I hope no one finds out yet. I don't want them to know I'm looking for another job. This time I'd like my personal business to stay private.

***

I had driven downtown to the Baltimore City Public Schools office one day after school a few months prior. I left straight from school and didn't miss any time off work. I usually stayed after school to clean up and get ready for the next day, but on this particular day I left immediately after the students. I dressed a little nicer than usual, but since I wore a dress every day, nobody paid attention. Nor did they notice that I left earlier than usual.

When I had interviewed with the county, the interviewer had a book with specific questions in it, and as I answered, she made notes and scored me. I must not have scored well, because they didn't offer me a job. When I interviewed with the city, the lady asked me the standard interview questions and a few questions about my current teaching position. I didn't feel stressed at all. I was more stressed about driving and parking downtown. The interviewer was quite pleasant and didn't keep me waiting. When I left, I felt cheerful and confident. I hadn't heard from them for months. I had almost forgotten about it until I received that phone call.

***

My interview with the principal of this city school was on the southeast side of town. It took me the better part of an hour to travel around the beltway loop to get there. I had to go through a tunnel and pay a toll. I felt like I was driving out-of-state. I hadn't realized this school was so far away. Did I want to make this drive every day? To get out of my current school—yes, absolutely!

I was fortunate that I didn't have to take off work or give an excuse, since my interview was scheduled on a professional study day where I could leave school early. It was also a professional study day in the city, so there were no students in the building.

The principal was an older black gentleman who spoke with authority. He had a loud, clear voice which I would find out later would boom over the loudspeaker every morning. He had wrinkles, curly dark hair and large gold-rimmed glasses. He reminded me of Little Richard, the musician from the 1950s and 1960s. He was spry, and his petite frame bounced around the school when he was out and about. I was told he had been the principal for so many years that he'd probably retire soon. I didn't realize that most of the staff wanted him to retire. But he surprised everyone by continuing for many more years. This man wasn't slowing down anytime soon.

It didn't seem like an interview. It was a very short meeting, and I got the impression that he had already decided to hire me; this was just a formality. Perhaps the lady at the Baltimore City Public Schools office had talked highly of me. Or perhaps he just really needed to fill a position.

I wondered how many applicants he had for this job, but this time I didn't ask. I was happy to be in a school that was more like what I was accustomed. The main office had multiple secretaries who were using updated equipment. The principal's office did not have a large, leather sofa. I didn't get a tour of the school nor meet any other staff, and I didn't care. I was just happy to be in a different environment.

When the assistant principal called me at home a week later to formally offer me the job, I gladly accepted. I always wanted to teach in a public school. I knew that teaching in a city school wasn't ideal, but I was willing to put up with whatever problems they had so that I could leave the anti-Semitism behind. I wasn't sure how to tell the people at the Catholic School I was leaving. I felt they expected me to stay there for years, as most of the faculty had done. I don't know how they could have expected that given how I had been treated.

***

The school year had ended, but staff was required to be there several days after. All the teachers were cleaning up and storing things. Mrs. A came in my room with instructions for how to store textbooks. I was afraid to tell her, but after listening to her directions, I told her that I accepted a job in Baltimore City Public Schools.

"What?"

"I took a job in the city," I repeated.

"You're leaving?"

"Yes. I'm not coming back next year."

"Does Mr. Z know this?"

"Yes, I already told him."

"Oh. Why would you do that? Why would you leave?"

"I got a better offer."

"Oh. I don't really get it," she muttered on her way out.

Well, at least she didn't give me a hard time about it. But she could have said something positive such as wishing me luck.

That afternoon the middle school teachers had a meeting in the science lab. I planned to make an announcement. I had already handed the principal a formal resignation letter. He read it immediately and thanked me for the notice. He didn't look surprised or upset.

The science teacher was asking, "So how do we want to do the schedule for next year?"

I asked Mrs. H, "Why are we already planning next year's schedule?"

"So we don't have to come in over the summer to figure it out. We make the schedule for the middle school ourselves."

Really? You do that too? The school secretary or the principal doesn't do that? I never realized that before. I wasn't involved with that last year.

As with most meetings, I didn't say much. I sat there trying to determine when and how to tell them I wasn't

235

returning. The meeting went on, and I didn't want to interrupt. Every time there was a pause in the conversation, I opened my mouth to speak, but someone interjected and I gave up. I guess I was also being a "chicken."

"Go ahead, Diane. Tell them your news," Mrs. A declared very loudly and clearly from behind me.

I turned and looked at her.

"Go ahead and tell them your big news. Say it."

They all looked at me.

"Yes. I was trying to find the right time. I guess there is no good time. I accepted a job in Baltimore City for next year."

After a brief, somewhat stunned silence, the science teacher was the first to speak.

"Congratulations, Diane. We all sincerely wish you the very best."

"Thank you."

"Yes," the others chimed in, except for Mrs. A.

Mrs. A rose from her seat and walked to the door.

"I'm going to find Mr. Z. This isn't right. You can't just leave like this."

Now it was my turn to sit in stunned silence.

"Oh, she'll get over it," Mrs. H, the religion teacher, said after Mrs. A left.

"Yes, she'll get over it," the social studies teacher agreed. "Diane, why don't you go pack up your stuff? You must have plenty to do."

"Yes, thanks." I was glad to get out of there.

Mrs. A ducked her head into my room at the end of the day before she left.

"By the way, you are not to use my back door to take your things out of the building. I don't want you going through my room."

"Oh...okay."

"You got it, right? No taking your stuff out my door."

"Yes, I understand."

What the heck? How mean was that?! It was a long way around the building to the front door for me to carry all my stuff, and some of my materials are heavy and bulky. I had hundreds of books to take home too. Her door was right off the parking lot. Why on earth would she prohibit me from using it? I didn't do anything wrong. I'm certainly allowed to resign my position. Some people don't even wait until the end of the year to quit. I stayed through an entire school year before I resigned. Her actions were just resentful. I wonder what she said to the principal.

Mrs. E came to my room about an hour later.

"Diane, I heard what Mrs. A said, and you are welcome to take your belongings out my door instead."

"Thank you so much."

"It's no problem."

Thank goodness! Mrs. E had the room adjacent to Mrs. A and was also off the parking lot. While it wasn't as convenient, it was a big help. I wonder how Mrs. E heard. Did Mrs. A tell everybody every single thing? Does she just stand in the middle of a crowd and complain and vent about me? Or Did Mrs. E happen to overhear? Or did someone else overhear and pass along the information like one big rumor mill? What did I care? I didn't have to lug my belongings all the way around the building.

After school ended, I still had access to the building. Several days later, my dad brought his van and helped me load everything in order to make fewer trips. We took everything out Mrs. E's door. I was glad nobody was around. I didn't want to talk to anyone or say goodbye.

On my last trip, I stopped in front of the Virgin Mary and observed her for another minute or two.

"Goodbye, Mary. You're actually not that bad to look at it, even though I didn't really want you looking over my shoulder every day for the last two years. You saw a lot. You witnessed most of my time here. If you could talk, I wonder what you'd say. How about 'Diane, you did a fine job. In the name of the Father, Son and Holy Spirit, this school doesn't realize what they are losing. Go fair child into the world. Go with my blessing. Amen.'"

I laughed at myself and shut the door behind me.

I never told my parents all the things that happened. But I knew when we drove away, my father was thrilled. He had suggested he bring his van to get all my belongings. I think he wanted to get me out of there as quickly as possible. Had he any clue what I had been through?

Chapter 20

Courage to change the things I can

Teaching in a public city school was exactly what one would expect. It was more challenging dealing with student behavior instead of parent behavior. In spite of the problems, I was still happy to be out of the Catholic school.

I ran into Mrs. H in the local McDonald's later that year, and she told me that when Mrs. A had stormed out of our meeting to complain to the principal about me leaving, she had said to him that it was wrong of me to resign on such short notice, and that he should have charged me the $500 fine for breaking my contract since I had already signed on the dotted line and committed to the next school year.

Really? Short notice? They had the whole summer to replace me. Charge me the $500 fine? Really? They paid me so little as it was, that would be a downright slap in the face! At least he had the courtesy not to enforce that stupid rule.

She told me that Mr. Z had said to Mrs. A, "Really? Don't you see that she's 'jumping from the frying pan into the fire'?"

I wasn't sure how I felt about this comment. Part of me was glad he realized how challenging my new job would be. But another part of me was angry that he compared his school to a frying pan and never did anything to turn down the heat.

Mrs. H also told me they hired a Catholic teacher in my place who was certified in Social Studies. Mrs. H said the kids didn't like how she was teaching.

Well of course not. Teaching English is not the same as teaching Social Studies. Wasn't he considering a Social Studies teacher when he interviewed me? I wonder if she's the same person. I shouldn't feel happy that the kids don't like her. I don't want the kids to be unhappy. But I can't help feeling a little glad about it. I hope the kids complain to the principal and the other teachers. I hope that maybe someone feels sad that I'm not there. The staff must be happy that they found a Catholic teacher. I bet they'll never hire another Jew!

Mrs. H also said that Mrs. A had lent this new teacher her old bulletin boards.

Really? The ones she told me she disposed of so that she couldn't lend me anything? Really nice.

Mrs. H said that Mrs. A has been really nice to the new Catholic teacher and that they had become friends.

Of course. Mrs. A is happy to have a fellow Catholic. I'm sure she won't slam the door on this lady and leave her out in the cold during parent-teacher conferences. It's not surprising that they're fast friends. Mrs. A probably has her over to dinner. They must be bosom buddies.

Mrs. H gave me the date of graduation and encouraged me to come. She said that my former seventh graders who were now graduating eighth graders would love to see me. I couldn't resist. I still missed them. I had to go celebrate and wish them well. After all, I never said goodbye.

I didn't have school that day, so I was able to go without taking time off. I didn't know where they'd be holding the service, so I walked through the front door. The school secretary greeted me warmly and directed me to the new church. I did my lap around the building. I peeked through the window of my former classroom, but it was dark and empty. I couldn't see anything. I tried the doorknob, but the room was locked.

Darn. I just wanted to see it again. I wonder how it's decorated. I'm sure the seating arrangement has changed. I really wanted to see which of Mrs. A's bulletin boards was on the wall.

As I approached the vestibule of the new church, all the teachers were gathered. A few said hello.

Mrs. A smiled, said "Hi, Diane," and gave me a big hug.

Wow. Is she really happy to see me? If she isn't, she is a really good faker.

"Oh, you got your hair cut!" I exclaimed. She had one of those short, snazzy cuts that looked like it had to be blow dried every morning. It was nicely done and complimented her face.

"Yes, I did."

"Well it looks great!"

"Thanks."

Some of the teachers standing behind me were grinning when I turned around. I even thought I detected two of them winking at each other. Was Mrs. A making faces over my shoulder while she was hugging me? Was she sticking her tongue out or rolling her eyes? Maybe she looked like she was going to gag because she really couldn't stand me. Or did those other teachers have inside jokes about me? I hope I read the situation incorrectly.

Mrs. A walked away, and that was the last time I saw her. I don't know where she sat in the sanctuary. I looked around for her afterward to say goodbye. She probably made it a point to avoid me after the service.

I found a seat by myself on an empty bench toward the back. Now it was evident how alone I felt there. But I wasn't alone for long. I had a feeling one of my former students would come over to say hello. I just didn't know which one. I was surprised by who it was.

I sensed a person sitting next to me as I looked in the prayer book. When I looked up, it was Greg.

"Hello, Ms. B," he said, hugging me warmly. I wanted to cry. After all we had been through, I felt particularly close to him, and it appeared he felt the same.

"Greg, what are you doing here? You already graduated."

"My sister is graduating this year."

"Why of course! How could I forget? How are you and your family?"

"We're all good."

I loved having his sister in my class my second year. She was a sweet child and a hard worker.

"How are you, Ms. B?"

"I'm good. Thanks for asking."

"Do you like your new school? What grades do you teach? Is it like here?"

"It's very different, since I'm in a public school. I'm teaching grades 7 and 8 this year. It's nothing like here. The kids don't go to church, and there are a lot more students. They are nothing like any of you. Nobody could compare to you anyway. Teachers aren't supposed to have favorites, but you all will always be my favorite students, especially your class. Just please don't tell anyone I said that!"

"I won't say a thing. It's good to see you, Ms. B. I have to go."

He scooted down the pew and back to his seat closer to the front. Tears welled up in my eyes, and I had a lump in my throat. I didn't get paid much and I put up with a lot of aggravation and adult bullying, but seeing these kids again, especially Greg, made it all worth it. I knew that I truly had made a difference.

Brooke came over to me next. I was so happy to see her, since she had left our school part way through the year. I found out that her family had to move because she had been sexually abused by a relative. She was such a lovely, sweet, friendly girl that it was heartbreaking for us to hear that. I had wondered what happened to her.

We embraced immediately. She was her warm, friendly self. I couldn't mention to her that I knew this information or ask any questions about it. So I just let her talk.

"Ms. B! How are you? It's so nice that you came back for graduation."

"Yes, I wouldn't miss it for the world! I'm so glad I could be here. And it's so good to see you."

"Yes, I didn't want to miss it either. I'm glad I get to say hello to my friends. I haven't seen everyone in a long while."

"Yes, we haven't seen you in some time."

"We didn't move that far away, but I had to go to public school."

"Do you like it? How's it going?"

"It's okay. It's just not the same as being here. I miss everybody."

"We really missed you too."

"I have to go. Take care, Ms. B."

"Take care, Brooke."

Thank heavens she seems to be doing well. Although obviously sometimes you never know what's really going on with someone. Thankfully, I think her family got her the help she needed. I always prayed that she would turn out okay.

During the service, as with past graduation ceremonies, the pastor asked the teachers to stand and be recognized. I thought I saw some glances in my direction, but I remained seated. I had not taught these kids the last school year, even though I had them for two years straight before then. Besides, I felt that if I stood I might enrage some of the parents who were against my presence from the start. I certainly didn't want to stir up any more controversy.

I didn't approach any graduates after the service, since they were all with their families, and I wasn't going to interrupt. I certainly didn't want to talk to any of the parents.

Once the service was over, a couple other kids came over to briefly say hello. Nadine told me how much they disliked the teacher who replaced me. Rather than write about their own interests, she forced them to complete writing exercises from the textbook. In addition, she had returned their writing folders to them. These folders contained all the writing they had completed in my class for two years. I considered these folders precious treasures as well as hard evidence of their growth as writers, readers, and students. I felt that this work and any future work should have been saved and returned to them upon graduation.

What would you expect from a Social Studies teacher with no experience teaching English Language Arts? That's an indication right there that she doesn't value their writing. Apparently she doesn't recognize the quality of their work. What a shame she doesn't acknowledge their good work and realize what they are capable of. Oh well. There's nothing I can do about it. I feel bad for the kids.

I must admit it didn't make me feel so bad that they didn't like my replacement!

Many of the kids acknowledged me with a wave or a smile. The important thing was that they knew I came back for them. I'm certain they all knew that I would always have that special teacher love for them.

Mrs. H came over to me.

"Ms. B, you'll come back for next year's graduation too, right?"

"Of course, I will. Thanks so much for letting me know when this was. Otherwise, I would have missed it entirely."

"No problem. Glad I ran into you that day."

"Yes, me too."

I ran into Mrs. H only one more time. She had taken a position in another Catholic school where she became principal. She said she was much happier.

I never saw most of those teachers again. I ran into Mrs. G, a lower school teacher, in a store one day about twenty five years later. She remembered me. Of course, her son is now married with children. She retired from the school after thirty years. She filled me in on what became of some of my eighth graders my first year. It was a thrill to hear about them.

I ran into the school secretary the same year in the grocery store. She was easy to recognize because she looks exactly the same! When I mentioned that we are members of a nearby synagogue, she said she didn't know I was Jewish!

"Really?" I asked. "Because we had a whole conversation about it when I was hired."

"No, I don't remember that."

How could she have forgotten? She didn't know the discrimination I faced?

Well, it was a long time ago. But I remember it all so vividly. I can never forget. A slogan Jews say regarding the Holocaust is "Never again." We're supposed to remember so we don't let persecution happen again.

Epilogue

And the wisdom to know the difference

Several years after I left that school, I went to a local club with a few girlfriends. I don't really like clubs, but this one was more upstanding, and we wanted to dance. There was a dance floor with a DJ and a bar area. They had regular tables, and patrons could order food and drinks. Even though it was crowded, we were able to find a table.

As we were seating ourselves, over the music I heard, "Ms. B, over here!" There was a familiar-looking stout lady waving to me from a table close by.

I walked over.

"Ms. B, do you remember us?" She was sitting with two other ladies.

"Of course, I do."

"How are you?"

"I'm good. How are all of you?"

"Good," she replied. "We're still working at the school in the cafeteria."

"Really? You've been there a long time."

"Yes, our kids aren't there anymore, but they still need the help."

Was I mistaken? Do these ladies get paid to work there? I'm not going to ask.

The second lady was smiling at me. I didn't remember her at all. The third lady was the blonde cafeteria lady— the one who despised me. Of course she was not smiling.

"Why don't you sit down and join us?" the first lady asked.

Are you kidding? Why would you want to socialize with me?

"No thanks, I'm here with friends," I replied. "Good seeing you."

I looked over at the blonde lady. She had that same disgusted, nasty look on her face as when she'd see me at school.

Does this one lady not know how much the other one hates me? Or is this some kind of joke? I can only imagine how the blonde cafeteria lady would have reacted if I sat down at her table.

I was happy to return to the table with my friends, those people who liked me and weren't disgusted by me. Never in a million years would I have sat with those women. As a matter of fact, I was so uncomfortable that I didn't want to dance in front of them. When my friends asked who they were, I told them they worked at my old school. I never told them of my tribulations. I was a very private person, and I kept a lot of things to myself. Maybe I would have benefitted by discussing it in the open. But I never wanted word to get back to anyone at the school that I was talking about them. I was also afraid that my friends might inadvertently tell my family, and I didn't want any family members to take it upon themselves to go to that school and complain. I felt that would just make the situation worse. Therefore, I never spoke about it.

When those ladies left the night club, I got up to dance.

***

In 2008, my cousin David married a Catholic woman. They were married in a Catholic church, and my father refused to attend. I knew my dad wasn't going to set foot in a church. And he wasn't thrilled about the marriage either. It made me uncomfortable that he wouldn't go, but he gave some other excuse. By this time I was married, and my husband and I went.

They had a beautiful wedding. The church sanctuary was magnificent, although not quite as big or modern as that of the new church at my former school. It was painted off-white and had high ceilings and stained glass.

I chuckled.

"What's so funny?" my husband asked.

"Here I am sitting in a Catholic church again after all these years. Only this time half the people here are Jewish. How do you feel about being in a church? Do you think it bothers anybody else?"

"No, it doesn't bother me. It's just a wedding. It doesn't seem to bother anybody else either," he said turning his head to look around at the occupants of the sanctuary.

My relatives were sitting up front while we were in the back, so I couldn't speak to them. The bride and groom walked down the long aisle and up the steps to the altar.

They lit tall, elaborate candles as part of the ceremony. At the end, the minister proclaimed them husband and wife.

Thank goodness my father didn't come. He'd hate this. They didn't use a rabbi, break the glass, sip the wine, say any of the blessings, or do anything from a traditional Jewish ceremony. I'm surprised. I thought they would have put some Jewish elements in there.

The reception was held in a restaurant. My husband and I were seated at a table for two during the cocktail hour when a gentleman came up to us.

"Pardon me. I had to come over. My wife thinks she knows you. She said that you are Ms. B, but I said she is wrong. Are you a teacher by any chance?"

"Why, yes, I am! I'm Ms. B."

Obviously they know me from my teaching days. Hmm...he doesn't look familiar. Who are they? I'm not going to tell them my married name. If they happen to be from the Catholic school, I don't want them to look me up. You never know what can happen. I guess I'm still paranoid.

"I'm Michael Bingham's dad. My wife is over there," he said, pointing across the room.

Yes, they are parents of one of my former Catholic school students. It looks like the mother doesn't want to come over and say hello.

"Wow! Thanks for saying hello. This is my husband. How is Michael? He must be—How old is he now?"

"He's 32, and that's him at the table with my wife. He's the one with all that hair on top of his head. I wouldn't expect you to recognize him. We're not fans of the hair bun!"

Michael looked nothing like the short kid with the round eyeglasses that I remembered. This tall man had no spectacles at all.

"Oh my gosh!! You're right. I wouldn't have recognized him at all! Do you mind if I say hello?"

He waved his son over before I could walk over to him.

Holy cow! His wife sees her son coming over to me, but she isn't smiling or waving hello. I can't believe this. I haven't taught at that school in years. Is she still holding a grudge against me?

Michael stood next to his dad and was about a foot and a half taller. I leaned my head back to look up at him.

"Oh, my gosh! Michael, I can't believe it's you! How are you?"

I didn't attempt to hug him since there was such a height difference between us. Plus, I wasn't sure how that would be received by his parents.

"Hi, Ms. B. I'm fine. How are you?"

"I'm good, thank you."

"How is everything?"

"Everything is good. It's good to see you, Ms. B. If you'll excuse me, I have to get back."

Michael returned to his mother.

Well that was just uncomfortable and disappointing. I wanted to talk to him so much more. What did Michael do with himself? What is he doing now? Does he have a job, a career, a profession? His dad could have bragged about him a little and told me something. That was a terrible conversation, if you'd even call it that. I wonder if he cut the conversation short because his mom didn't want him to come over.

At least Michael's dad was pleasant. He didn't have to come over and say hello unless the curiosity was killing him. I still don't remember his wife, but maybe she was friends with the blonde cafeteria lady. I hope that I am misreading the situation, and she has an injury that won't allow her to get up and walk over. But wouldn't he have said?

Months after the wedding, I was talking to my cousin David and his new wife, and I told them how Mr. Bingham had recognized me as his son's former teacher. It turns out that Mr. Bingham was the bride's uncle!!

That's her uncle!!! Oh my goodness! I'm glad I didn't say anything else about Mr. Bingham and his wife. She's obviously close to him. I certainly don't want to say anything negative.

And how about that?! The Binghams are now related to a Jew!! A family from my former Catholic school now has a branch on a Jewish family tree!

I really have to ruminate over this one. How times have changed. So many Jewish people have intermarried. So many people all over the world have married outside of their own faith. I wonder how many more instances there are of this in my former Catholic school community.

This reminds me of a story my father told about when he attended a dinner with my mother's family early in their marriage and had to sit next to a Japanese man. My father had commented, "During the war I was killing them, and now I'm breaking bread with them." He couldn't believe that when he was a young man, he had to shoot Japanese soldiers during World War II, and later in life he was sitting down to a meal with Japanese people. How uncomfortable that must have been for him. That's how uncomfortable I feel every time I come across certain people from this school. I guess that will never change.

Times change and hopefully relationships improve, including those around the world. I mentioned Hitler and the Nazi Regime to Greg when I attempted to briefly review a history of anti-Semitism. Unfortunately, as he and I spoke, there were more horrific events unfolding in another part of the world. In the former Yugoslavia, "ethnic cleansing" was taking place. While Jews were not the target in this case, Bosnian Muslims were. Thousands of people were being tortured and murdered because of their ethnicity, much like the Jews in the Holocaust. There should be no place in this world where hatred, prejudice, bigotry, racism, anti-Semitism, or any type of discrimination can prevail. Nor should there ever be a place in our very own communities where this is permitted. Unfortunately, we still see it today in current news events. This is one "disease" that is proving difficult to eradicate throughout the world.

Perhaps instances of intermarriage will help build a world where religious differences are no longer an issue. I hope that intermarriage between different religions, races, and nationalities affect tolerance and acceptance of people all over the world. Perhaps relationships can improve in other ways as well. Maybe one day everyone will be accepting of all people. And may there be peace throughout the world, forever and always. Amen.

***

In 2018 I received a Facebook message from Greg:
Miss B? I don't know if you remember me. You taught me English in 8th grade. I just wanted to tell you that even though it was so long ago, I never forgot you. You were

my greatest teacher. I don't mean English, either. You taught me tolerance and forgiveness, and I want to say thank you for having an impact on my life.
(Reprinted with permission)

I can't read this message without crying. What else can be said? This is my greatest reward, the Nobel prize of teaching. I can walk away knowing I did something good in this world. The Talmud (Jewish scripture) teaches that, "Whoever destroys a soul, it is considered as if he destroyed an entire world. And whoever saves a life, it is considered as if he saved an entire world." Just maybe I saved a life. I hope you will too.

Discussion Questions

1. What was Ms. B's motivation for teaching in the Catholic school? Do you think it was justified?
2. Do you believe Ms. B should have been teaching in the Catholic school? Support your rationale.
3. Could you see the viewpoint of the teachers, parents and staff who were against Ms. B teaching in the school? How did they feel? Might you have felt the same way if you were in their position?
4. Which behaviors do you think were based in anti-Semitism and which were not? Explain.
5. Ms. B states that she was not going to decorate for Christmas, Kwaanza, and Chanukah. She did not have it in her to fight for it. Why was this? What would you have done? Do you think she should have fought for it?
6. While Ms. B had teaching experience, she was not an experienced teacher. Do you think it would have been different for her if she was? How so?
7. Ms. B admits that she was naive. Where do you think her naiveté appears in the story? How might those instances have been different if she had been more shrewd and worldly?
8. What did you think of the character of Greg? Christopher? Were they responsible for their actions? Should they have received consequences for their actions? If so, what and by whom? Do you think Ms. B dealt with them appropriately?
9. Who did you feel were the antagonists in the story? Why? How did you feel about their actions?

10. What experiences have you had where you could relate to the main character, Ms. B? Have you ever felt like "a fish out of water" or "the odd man out"? When?

11. Do you think anyone in the story tried to do "the right thing"? Who? Why?

12. What did you think of the chapter titles? Were they appropriate? Why or why not?

13. What did you think of the author's views about the future at the end of the story? Do you agree or disagree? Why? How do you feel about the changes that have happened?

14. What did you think of the principal, Mr. Z? Should he have done anything differently? What do you think his feelings were toward Ms. B? Do you think he was influenced by Mrs. A?

15. Is this school like any place you know? Do you feel that you are aware of an institution, organization, company or group who behaves this way toward outsiders? Explain.

16. What might you have done differently if you were Ms. B when:
    - She received the note the first day
    - The parent refused to let the child serve detention
    - She went to church

17. Was there any other instance you know you would have handled differently?

18. Did you find anything in the story humorous? Which parts? Why?

19. Can you relate to any part of the story as an educator, child care provider, or other worker who deals with children? Explain.

20. Do you think it is important for children to be taught religion? To be taught religion in school? In a religious school setting? At home? Why or why not? How do you think these children were taught religion? Do you think it was effective? Why or why not?

21. What did you think of Ms. B returning for a second year of teaching? Would you have?
22. Do you think Ms. B's own religious beliefs played any part in any decisions she made or in any of her behaviors?
23. Do you feel any of the parents overreacted at any point in the story? If so, when? Was it justified?
24. Do you think Ms. B's long-term absence due to medical reasons was handled appropriately by the school? Explain.
25. Are you a religious person? Do you subscribe to a particular religion? How would your religious beliefs guide you in this situation?
26. Why do you think Ms. B received so many Christmas presents? Get-well cards? What did you think of her reaction to each? What did you think of the Secret Santa gift exchange?
27. What did you think of the Saturday detention? The detention policy?
28. Did you think any of the rules or practices should have been changed for Ms. B? Why or why not?
29. What kind of a teacher was Ms. B? How would you have felt if she was your teacher? Would you have wanted her for a teacher? Why or why not?
30. What did you think of the oratorical contest? Should it have been an annual event? Why or why not?
31. What was your impression of the school as a whole? Would you enroll your child? Why or why not?
32. How do you think the story would have been different if it occurred today?

Acknowledgments

"Would you just take, along with me, 10 seconds to think of the people who have helped you become who you are, those who cared about you and wanted what was best for you in life."

— Fred Rogers in his acceptance speech for the Lifetime Achievement Award in 1997

This book would never have come to fruition were it not for Professor Jacob Lampell at the Community College of Baltimore County. He worked with me in a self-directed class to study memoir writing, encouraged me to add more of myself to the story, and brought out the best in my writing.

Thank you to my friends at the Baltimore Jewish Writers Guild for their support and critiques of many chapters of this book. The longtime members are Linda Miller, Mark Carp, Edy Bondroff, Marlene Solomon, Laurie Cohen, and Ada Strausberg. Terri Kane, we still miss having you as our leader. Thank you especially to my dear friend Linda for the many hours she took to review every chapter outside of our writing group.

Thank you to my husband for being my partner throughout this process. Your business acumen in particular came in handy.

I benefited from a memoir writing class taught at the Jewish Community Center by guest instructor, Leslie Atkins. I enjoyed the company of other memoir writers and honed my writing skills.

I owe a debt of gratitude to local author, Michael Olesker, for being the first to review my work. I truly appreciate your guidance and willingness to help a first-timer.

Many thanks to Apprentice House Press led by director Kevin Atticks for selecting my manuscript. I wish all the best to the competent and capable students in the communications department at Loyola University.

A big hug is extended to my former student known in this book as Greg. Our bond will never be broken. You have more insight and understanding than most. I hope you never change, and I always wish you well.

About the Author

Diane Gensler is a certified English and special education teacher. In addition to teaching in public and private schools, she developed educational software, tutored online and wrote and managed online curriculum. She is a Maryland Writing Project Teacher Consultant and a mentor. A native Baltimorean and mother of three, she is an active member of multiple Parent Teacher Associations, the Baltimore Jewish Writers Guild, the Jewish Genealogy Society of Maryland and other clubs and organizations.

Apprentice
House Press
Loyola University Maryland

Apprentice House is the country's only campus-based, student-staffed book publishing company. Directed by professors and industry professionals, it is a nonprofit activity of the Communication Department at Loyola University Maryland.

Using state-of-the-art technology and an experiential learning model of education, Apprentice House publishes books in untraditional ways. This dual responsibility as publishers and educators creates an unprecedented collaborative environment among faculty and students, while teaching tomorrow's editors, designers, and marketers.

Outside of class, progress on book projects is carried forth by the AH Book Publishing Club, a co-curricular campus organization supported by Loyola University Maryland's Office of Student Activities.

Eclectic and provocative, Apprentice House titles intend to entertain as well as spark dialogue on a variety of topics. Financial contributions to sustain the press's work are welcomed. Contributions are tax deductible to the fullest extent allowed by the IRS.

To learn more about Apprentice House books or to obtain submission guidelines, please visit www.apprenticehouse.com.

Apprentice House
Communication Department
Loyola University Maryland
4501 N. Charles Street
Baltimore, MD 21210
Ph: 410-617-5265
info@apprenticehouse.com
www.apprenticehouse.com

9 781627 202831